New School – Skiing's Next Generation

NEW SCHOOL
SKIING'S NEXT GENERATION

BABIC/BLÖCHL/BLÖCHL

MEYER
& MEYER
SPORT

Original title: New School – Faszination auf Skiern
© 2005 by Meyer & Meyer Verlag, Aachen
Translated by Heather Ross

British Library Cataloguing in Publication Data
A catalogue record for this book is available from the British Library

New School – Skiing's Next Generation
Oxford: Meyer & Meyer Sport (UK) Ltd., 2006
ISBN 10: 1-84126-180-7
ISBN 13: 978-1-84126-180-5

© 2006 by Meyer & Meyer Sport (UK) Ltd.
Aachen, Adelaide, Auckland, Budapest, Graz, Johannesburg,
New York, Olten (CH), Oxford, Singapore, Toronto
Member of the World
Sports Publishers' Association (WSPA)
www.w-s-p-a.org
Printed and bound by: B.o.s.s Druck und Medien GmbH, Germany
ISBN 10: 1-84126-180-7
ISBN 13: 978-1-84126-180-5
E-Mail: verlag@m-m-sports.com
www.m-m-sports.com

CONTENTS

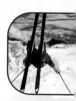

Warning!

1 FOREWORD

Since the origin of skiing, long before the current obsession with time and distance, skiers have tried to develop their own unique style and technique. This trend runs right through the history of skiing to the present day, starting with the Norwegians in 1820, followed by Arthur Fuhrer in Switzerland, the Hotdoggers in the '70s and '80s and now the new freestyle and freeskiing sports of today.

Every film that ski film producers, such as Warren Miller, Willi Bogner or Matchstick Productions MSP, make fires our imaginations with spectacular images of jumps against a backdrop of impressive natural scenery. Almost every ski resort has a terrain park that is used by both snowboarders and skiers.

But how can Joe Average do a stylish trick like the "pros" in the Free Ski magazines and films? Just taking off and trusting to chance and good luck, hoping that you land on your feet like a cat is certainly very brave, but doing this will make you much more likely to gain the sympathy of the nurse in the local hospital than gaining the admiration on the slopes.

Complex jumps like the 360°, flips and spins are supposedly far too difficult for most skiers to learn. This book is intended to prove the contrary. It describes how different jumps can be learned easily and quickly.

Methodical teaching methods and graphic photo sequences give beginners all the information they need for their first jump with easy grabs or 360°s. This book shows experienced skiers how to do jumps like the Fly Away Front Flip, Back Flip and Loop Side Flip and, for the very best, there are descriptions of the Rodeo 540° and the Misty. There are plenty of instructions and drills that make it easy to learn the new jumps and also to keep the risk of injury as low as possible. There are also tips for adapting the jumps you have learned to your favorite terrain, whether it is in the backcountry over cliffs or on the Big Air Kickers in the terrain park, in the halfpipe or even on the moguls.

www.davidbabic.com

1.1 Introduction and Presentation of the Authors

The term New School is now established among skiers. The ski industry uses it to describe the new skiing disciplines of halfpipe, Big Air and slopestyle events in terrain parks. New School elements have also been incorporated in the Olympic discipline of moguls, so it is not surprising that the French call the New School movement New Freestyle. The term Freeski is frequently used incorrectly, as it actually means off-piste skiing. The boundaries are fluid though, as many "freeskiers" can also be found in the park and "New Schoolers" off-piste.

Ski manufacturers report that the number of skis purchased that can be used for both Freeski and New School, which are called twintips, has risen dramatically. They benefit from the completely new, young, up-to-the minute image of the New School movement.

The new skis could not have equaled this image boost based solely on their technical aspects, such as their carving ability.

The ski industry currently enthralls ski fans with fantastic action images that fill the Free Ski magazines, advertising brochures and short films. They feature breathtaking jumps by Freeski and New School pros and often portray the image that with the right equipment anyone could do the same thing. This is definitely not the case; this sport can be very dangerous without instruction and a methodical progression. In fact, if you look at many of the top athletes currently leading this progression you will see that many of these individuals have a resume that began in ski racing, competitive mogul skiing, or some form of gymnastics that has given them a strong foundation to build upon.

Together, with my brother and with the help of David Babic, a current U.S. Ski Team member, I have made a compilation of personal experiences, tips and tricks. Together, we have worked out how to offer those who want to learn the safest introduction to this unique sport using a simple, methodical procedure. We have restricted ourselves to the so-called Basic Tricks, which we have photographed using small jumps. We didn't want to show any particularly difficult shots but instead sought to illustrate that, after practicing the right moves, many tricks can be performed from any small jump.

We want to touch on the special styles that definitely have an important place in this sport. This is the job of the authors of Free Ski magazines, photographers and filmmakers. Along with the pro performers, they give direction to and define the lifestyle of the sport by deciding which jump is hip or the most stylish. We just want to provide some building blocks from which the basic elements can be learned. Everyone must develop his or her own individual style. We don't want to get into judging or defining which trick is stylish or uncool. Before we get more involved in the subject of the book, and also consult international experts, we would like to introduce ourselves to the readers with a short personal biography.

David Babic
U.S. Ski Team Member
(www.davidbabic.com)

I, David Babic, was born and raised in Washington, Vermont. I am 26 years old and have been skiing competitively for the past 10 years. When I was young, my father decided that he would introduce his children to the wonderful world of skiing when we each turned 10 years old. This was the case for my two brothers, but I was resilient and begged to be taken along. So at 8 years old I strapped on my first pair of skies and was determined to keep up with my father and older brothers. This was the trend for many years, and I still believe that I carry this same determination and excitement for this sport that is still a big part of my life today.

I never really thought much about competition (besides the never-ending one between my brothers) until I watched Canadian Jean-Luc Brassard collect a gold medal in the '94 Olympics. I remember thinking right then, "This is what I want to do"! I was inspired by the way he took my family's weekend pasttime and lifted it to this exciting, admirable, almost superhuman-like art form. I, too, wanted to inspire others with my skiing in this way and to enjoy the feeling of seamless turns and effortless-looking jumps.

Soon after the Olympic games, this became my quest; I enrolled in Nick Preston's freestyle skiing program at Waterville Valley, NH, and began my competitive career. A few years later, under the guidance of coach Brian McNamara, I moved to Breckenridge, CO, to continue the development of my skills. In this region, I met many of the current U.S. Ski Team members. Athletes like Toby Dawson, Luke Westerlund, Jeremy Bloom, and Travis Mayer were common regional competitors, and our friendships and competition have grown through the years. Under the keen eye of Team Breckenridge coach Jon Dowling, I was able to refine my skills against this strong competition and set the table for ensuing success. I earned a spot on the U.S. Freestyle Ski Team in 2002, just after the Olympic games. For the past four years, I have had the amazing opportunity to compete on the World Cup Tour against some of the best athletes in the world. I received my first World Cup podium during the '03 Season in Steamboat Springs, CO. I then followed that season with my first World Cup Win in Airolo, Sui. I continue to push my own level by making technical changes in my skiing, not to mention performing the first ever off-axis 1080° spin in a World Cup competition. It is my hope that I can somehow pass on to others some of the knowledge, inspiration, and passion that skiing has provided for me. We are only as great our imagination. Chase those dreams!

David Babic

I, Gerhard Blöchl, am 23 years old and have been doing the sport for 7 years. Since my 16th birthday, as a member of the German National Ski Freestyle Team, I have spent about 200 days a year in the snow. Back in 1998, with my brother and our friend Nico Michel, a cameraman, we made a short film for the ski company Kneissl & Friends, in which we showed what the sport of Freeski is really like, with powder snow sequences and new school elements as part of a nice little story. This brought me to the attention of the American ski company K2, which then invited me to join its international free ski team.

This eventually led to a collaboration with Si-Q, which sponsors a variety of young talents in the sport and music business, and without whose support this book would never have been published. In the past couple of years, my work has increasingly focused on my core discipline of moguls, so it is all the more pleasant for me that I can now live my passion for New School in an Olympic discipline, for overhead and off-axis jumps have been allowed in moguls since 2002. The 2002-3 season was also my first World Cup season. My best results up to now have been a 13th place in Steamboat, U.S.A., and a 9th place in the Dual in Madarao, Japan. But I am happiest about my 15th place in the World Championships in Deer Valley, U.S.A., and both my German titles in the spring of 2004.

My brother Armin competed in European Cup Mogul races for Germany before I did and later took part in several Freeski competitions. However, in 1999 he decided to concentrate on his studies and has worked as a sports teacher for the past two years. He is now able to help me with advice on a practical level in my activities; he takes photographs and advises me as a coach.

Gerhard Blöchl

*Gerhard Blöchl (www.bloechl.com)
World Cup skier and two-time
German champion, Ski Freestyle*

*Armin Blöchl, sports teacher,
*C-Trainer Ski Freestyle
Photo: Doris Huber*

This book cannot and should not replace the experience and advice of an experienced coach who is able to give the skier his personal attention. But as increasing numbers of skiers are attempting jumps in the terrain parks of ski resorts – inspired by the spectacular images in ski magazines – it is the right time to give them all a practically oriented book.

1.2 Interview with World Champion Nathan Roberts

- **Gold medalist in the Ruka World Championship in 2005**
- **Multiple Ski Freestyle World Cup winner**

First, we all want to congratulate you on your recent World Championship win! This is a title that has eluded American men in Freestyle Moguls for many years. What was that experience like for you?

Winning World Championships was a childhood dream of mine since the age of 10. I began skiing moguls at the age of five. My mother would drop me off, and I would be off exploring the mountain trailing behind such Freestyle greats as two-time Olympian Craig Rodman and Sean Smith. From day one, they took me under their wings and showed me how it was done. This is where it all began and here I am today with my dream of becoming World Champion accomplished. What an incredible honor to wear that title.

As a young competitor, you've had a very successful career at the World Cup level, earning multiple World Cup wins, ranking in the top three in the World Cup overall, and now have a World Championship win. To what would you attribute to this astounding success?

I would first have to attribute most of my success to the support of my family and friends. I began skiing at the age 3 and competing at the age of 7, and although I didn't come from a wealthy family, they always found a way to make it possible for me to continue skiing. Many say that I was a late bloomer, as I had the talent, but it took a while for me to harness my potential to put together the full package. Although I made the U.S. Ski Team at the age of 18, I only held onto my spot for a year. It was really hard losing my spot as I still had these big goals. I look back now and realize that it was a true gift, as I really needed that time to refine my skills. A year later, I regained my position on the USST and have steadily worked my way up. Every year, I work harder to refine my skills both mentally and physically. Winning World Championships in Ruka was a culmination of my strong will, hard work, but mostly was due to the undying support of my family and friends.

It is true, that you competed in upright and inverted aerials as a junior level skier. With the recent FIS rule changes allowing mogul competitors to perform inverted maneuvers in competition, what advantages has this aerial background given you?

Yes, I competed in both upright and inverted aerials from 9-16 years of age. At that time, I was reaching a point in my career where I had to choose between aerials or moguls. Although I loved both events, in the end, the decision was not all that hard to make, my real passion was mogul skiing. Recently, FIS made inverted tricks legal in the moguls; prior to this, only tricks in which your feet did not go above your head were allowed. With this change, I feel that my aerial background has served to be a great advantage. Unlike the others who grew up simply skiing moguls and performing upright airs, I already had a jump on them. Instead of having to learn to go inverted at a later time in my career, I already had the know-how and the air awareness. With this, I was able to make the switch to inverted tricks in the moguls with both confidence and ease.

How do you feel about the way FIS competitions are currently scored? Would you like to see any changes in the future? Currently, many athletes are trying to performing difficult 720°s, 1080°s, back fulls, and back double-fulls, in competition. How do you feel about the direction in which athletes are currently pushing the sport? Would you like to see the sport focus on any additional tricks?

I would like to see the 'Free' put back in freestyle. Over the years, the sport of mogul skiing started to plateau as the tricks were not changing and many (myself included) began to see the sport becoming a bit boring. Jonny Moseley, who won the Gold in the '98 Olympics, was one of the leaders in our sport who not only took note of this but also decided to do something about it. He came into the 2002 Olympics doing a trick that made people stop dead in their tracks and take notice. He named the trick "The Dinner Roll," which was an off-axis 720. But the trick of it all was he had to stay within the FIS Guidelines and not let his legs go above his head. With this showing, a new revolution of mogul skiing began and inverted tricks came to the forefront of our sport. Four years later, with the 2006 Olympic year approaching, I have tried to revolutionize the sport once again. During the season, I have completed several double back flips in the moguls. I have submitted this trick to FIS, but it was strongly rejected. There was an agreement amongst many members of FIS that there would be NO new tricks issued on an Olympic year. Therefore, I would like to close with how I began; "I would like to see the 'free' put back in freestyle."

To conclude, do you have any advice for all our young New Schoolers and Freestylers?

Stay focused, follow your dreams, because dreams come true.

Thanks for having me for this interview,

Nate Roberts
USST

Thanks a lot from all our readers!

2 GENERAL PREREQUISITES

As already mentioned elsewhere, it is well known that these days nearly all ski resorts offer terrain parks with a halfpipe, a quarterpipe, rails and big air kickers. If you go to a small resort though, you can quickly dig a ramp in the snow for yourself just by using the natural formation of the ground. Self-built ramps are even better if you are a beginner, as they can be built to correspond exactly to your needs and the jumps you want to do.

This book contains tricks for anyone independent of his or her skiing ability. Basically, it is possible that even those who have only been skiing for a few weeks can learn a jump with skis if they want. However, the demands of the jump should always be adapted to the level of skiing experience. Someone who just wants to learn a few cool jumps only has to be able to hold a central body position over their skis to takeoff with the ability to control their landing after the jump. However, significantly more complex skiing ability is required if you are considering performing these jumps in the halfpipe, on the moguls or in rocky off-piste terrain.

Although this isn't a team sport, we do recommend that you train with friends or like-minded people. It is more fun in a group, you can share the work of digging a jump and if necessary give first aid more quickly if someone gets injured. When you are alone, you are not really aware of your mistakes, if at all, because you don't have a mirror in front of you, as a dancer does, for example, so that you can correct your movements yourself. In our sport, other people must act as a mirror, not only make suggestions as to how you can improve, but also preferably to film you with a video camera. It is often easy to misunderstand a well-meant suggestion and make the necessary improvement because not everyone is good at giving corrections. If this is the case, it is much better to analyze the video footage together.

If you want to perform New School jumps with skis, you should have your head firmly on your shoulders and first study the theoretical principles of learning the sport's movements. A basic knowledge of physics and sports psychology are also important. Although this may sound uncool, it will definitely help you a lot later on. Don't panic, you don't have to go back to high school; we always provide you with all the practical knowledge you need step by step in the explanations for each jump.

2.1 Basics

If you want to do this sport, bear in mind the following important principles of learning a new activity. This basic knowledge will not only protect you from injury but also help you to keep improving your jumps. In life, we frequently progress from the small to the large, from the simple to the complex.

It is absolutely necessary to acquire the basic skills on small jumps in order to keep to a certain methodical sequence. If you don't stick to this order, you are putting yourself at unnecessary risk and will often experience learning blocks because you lack elementary skills. That is why we want to actually learn about learning first.

Complex jumps with skis are learned in four steps.

These really elementary rules of learning should never be forgotten, for if you overestimate yourself and move on too quickly to the next step, you can hurt yourself very badly in many jumps. Courage is definitely an important prerequisite, but it must be used wisely. Injuries due overestimating your own ability can be avoided.

Four steps to learning complex jumps with skis:

Step 1: **Imagine the movement**
Good models help to provide a basic idea of the overall movement pattern. In practical terms, this means that you:
a) Watch films of the experts in slow motion
b) Study the important phases of a jump in sequential images, like the ones in this book.

Step 2: **Transfer into your movement patterns**
Using your own idea of the movement, try to execute the movement for the first time. The likelihood of you landing on your feet is probably less than 50%. That is why this stage should be carried out on a diving board into a pool, on a trampoline or a water ramp.

Step 3: **Transfer into a fine form**
To be prepared for this step, you must have already experienced the jumps yourself and know how to turn in space. As we are now going to move onto the snow ramps, the chances of a wipe out now have to be low. Landing on your feet should not be left to chance at this point. The probability should be 70-80%. At this stage, the saying "practice makes perfect" applies. To create the right conditions to perform the movement, please see chapter 2.4 "Ramp Construction" and Chapter 10 "Risk Management."

Step 4: **Automation of the movement/fine tuning**
Right from the first step, you will be able to jump from a diverse range of jumps. Your safety will ideally be up to 99%, and you can perform your trick successfully in most terrain parks.

2.2 Learning by Video

The video technique is a comparatively simple way of allowing you to monitor your learning progress and individual style effectively. For successful filming, you must choose the right equipment and stand in the right place. Research shows that it is a good idea to film the jump from several perspectives, as the footage can then be analyzed very accurately.

These could include looking from the side, from the front, the back and also from below, depending on the bravery of the cameraman, for this is really right in the center of the action instead of just next to it.

To start with, don't use the zoom too much, as it is much easier to follow the athlete and keep him in the field of vision. Ideally, the athlete should be at the center of the picture.

Just ask a friend to film you as you jump. You will get some nice clips and also a lot of information about what you are doing right or wrong in the jumps.

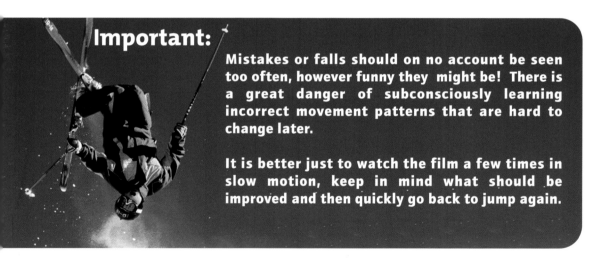

Important:

Mistakes or falls should on no account be seen too often, however funny they might be! There is a great danger of subconsciously learning incorrect movement patterns that are hard to change later.

It is better just to watch the film a few times in slow motion, keep in mind what should be improved and then quickly go back to jump again.

2.3 Equipment

You have probably been wondering what special equipment you will need for jumping. Theoretically, you can do a flip with any old wooden ski from your grandparents' attic. It is doubtful for how long though.

The question of equipment is not so easy to answer. It greatly depends on where you will use it, your weight and your preference. However, we will try to provide a summary of what is currently available on the market.

The Skis

The right ski model depends upon where it will be used. The choice of skis appropriate for different New School terrain depends on various criteria.

Use Twintips in the Park and Pipe.

Twintips possess two curved ends. This allows you to land and takeoff either forward or backward on the kicker. With skis without two tips, there is always the possibility that when you go backward that the flat end will get stuck in the snow. These skis are often constructed so that the binding is fixed more centrally compared to traditional skis, which can slightly spoil the general gliding performance of the skis. This binding position has practical advantages for tricks in the air, fakie, or when grinding on rails or other obstacles.

The length and stiffness of the skis depend on the skier's weight and height. We recommend that the skis reach the tip of your nose. Skis that are too short or too soft make landing and skiing after jumping from great heights more difficult. Anyone who has already tried to jump with ski boards or snow blades knows that it is almost impossible to land centrally enough on them so that you are able to avoid falling forward or backward in the snow.

As long as you don't want to compete in a skicross or giant slalom championships, the twintips are good comprehensive (all-around) skis, whose spatula shape and torsional stiffness mean that you can carve really well on the slopes. Their width also enables you to ski pretty well in powder snow.

If the skis are going to be used exclusively for jumping, they should be less shaped. Pronounced shaping always increases the risk of crashing when you land. Extremely waisted fun carvers should definitely not be used for jumping.

Use Mogul Skies on Moguls.

You can of course ski moguls with twintips or carving skis. If you want to take the sport more seriously though, you will need specialized mogul skis. Compared to carving skis, these are narrower and less waisted. This is important, as it enables you to avoid the skis touching each other or even crossing during a fast run down the moguls when your feet are close together. It is also worth mentioning that these special skis are usually very strong and will therefore last longer than standard models.

Mogul skis are produced by nearly every big ski manufacturer, but mainly for the North American and Japanese markets.

The length of the skis should be 5cm longer than your nose, but your first attempts will be easier with shorter skis. Short skis are not ideal for experts though, as for the above-mentioned reasons, landing and skiing are easier with longer skis. In the World Cup, most skiers use a length of 175-185cm.

Use Big Mountain Skies in Freeride Terrain.

Big Mountain skis are intended for the best skiing days of your life. They are the long boards that allow skiers to cruise smoothly in powder snow. Their wide construction gives unbelievable momentum on powder snow, where you can achieve breathtaking lines and speeds.

Although these kind of enormous skis have been regarded with some suspicion, they have now become more familiar and accepted. However, they still have a certain rarity   value in top resorts, such as Chamonix or La Grave.

sportOrange.com
sometimes it's better to have a coach!

The majority of skiers are still put off by the wide planks, as they are afraid they won't be able to control them. They would think differently though, if they only knew how well they work on soft and firm conditions. Even with Telemark bindings, skiing on powder or firm terrain becomes child's play. There are also more and more Big Mountain skis that are produced like twintips so that you can land one or two New School tricks backwards in the powder snow. The Freeride models should measure 20cm more than your body height.

The Binding

For normal skiing, the binding between the skier's foot and the ski should be firm and should loosen in case of a fall to protect the ankles and ligaments. That is why an individual position is needed for an ideal interaction between ski boot and binding. Like downhill racing skiers, New Schoolers and mogul skiers perform jumps that are subject to significantly higher forces than normal skiers.

This is why World Cup mogul skiers and New School and Freeski pros use a downhill racing binding. We advise against wedges and pads under the binding, for the same reason a woman would not do jumps in high heels. Wedges have a particularly negative effect on landing. As with strongly waisted skis, there is a high risk of getting dug into the snow.

 TIP Many people forget to unscrew the spring from the binding at the end of the season. Remembering to unscrew the binding spring makes the binding last longer, so that it will last for several years.

The Boots

When you choose a ski boot, the most important things are a good fit and no pressure points. If you really can't find a pair that fit, you can always make them fit by taking out the plastic shell or putting foam in the boot liner. The heavier the skier, the stiffer and harder the plastic shell should be.

The Poles

In the New School disciplines, poles are helpful for keeping balance and rhythm and, of course, for pushing off. You should not base your choice to buy on the color or grip design, but on the quality of the tube, so it is better to invest more money in a top-of-the-line product. Knowledgeable sales staff can advise you on the length, hardness and flexibility of the tubing. Bad quality sticks are a waste of time as they bend upon landing. We particularly recommend that you use sticks about 10cm shorter than normal.

The Helmet

More and more skiers are now wearing helmets. This is definitely advisable for the New School disciplines to avoid head injuries if you fall. The use of high-quality materials and new manufacturing technologies make it possible to develop very comfortable ski and snowboard helmets.

The New School and Freeski scene has helped considerably to make the wearing of helmets acceptable among young people, and they have even become stylish accessories. But when buying a helmet you should forget about fashion and color and ask yourself the following questions:

Can I wear my ski goggles with it?
Does it limit my field of vision?
Is the chinstrap padded or at least 1 in. wide?
Can I open the safety catch with gloves on?
Does the helmet wobble or cause pressure points?

The Goggles

You should choose goggles that fit your helmet and above all give you an unrestricted field of vision. There is nothing more unpleasant when doing a spin or skiing switch than having the frame of your goggles in your field of vision. Since the sport often makes you sweat more than you would expect, make sure that they are well ventilated.

The wearing of sunglasses when jumping is only provisionally recommended as there are hardly any models that don't slip off. It goes without saying that sunglasses should guarantee 100% UV protection and have unbreakable lenses. Good visibility is an important prerequisite for safe skiing.

Clothing

Good clothing should protect you both from getting cold and from overheating, be made from light and stretchy materials and be very comfortable to wear. It must also be resilient that the clothes don't tear easily if you fall. The textile industry manufactures clothes that meet all these demands. Special fibers and membranes, such as Gore Tex, fulfill all these functions and are water-, and windproof.

Good capillary conductivity of the inner fabric also takes the moisture produced during physical activity to the outside. We recommend that you wear several layers of clothing according to the onion principle so that you can remove or put on layers according to your needs and the weather conditions. The air between the layers also insulates the body so that you are able to ski even in very adverse weather conditions.

You should not buy clothes a size bigger just because it is trendy, but because it is practical – it allows you to wear protectors under your clothes.

Protectors

Our basic recommendations are a helmet and back protectors. There are many different kinds of protectors on the market, though, ranging from hip protectors with an integrated coccyx protector to back protectors to complete protective vests that provide total protection for the elbows, chest and spine, as worn for motorcross.

In spite of this, you must always bear in mind that safety can only be bought up to a certain point (see chapter 10 "Risk Management"). Protectors spread the forces acting on a small area over a slightly larger surface area and can alleviate the consequences of a fall, but not completely prevent them.

2.4 Ramp Construction

In terrain parks, there are different kinds of jumps that are not standardized. The one thing that they have in common is that they are built according to the physical principles of a flight path. The difference in height between the takeoff point and the landing should not be too great.

Photo: Armin Blöchl. Location: Zugspitze

For your first jumps, we recommend small ramps that you can build yourself and whose height you can increase step by step. When building a kicker in off-piste terrain, it is possible to use the natural features of the ground, thus saving yourself unnecessary shoveling! Make sure you build the ramp wide enough so that you can also do switch tricks safely. Loosely piled snow must be packed well by stepping firmly on the pile of snow with your skis.

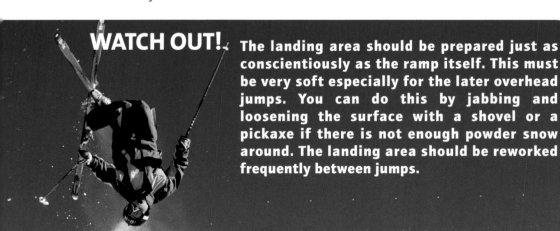

WATCH OUT! The landing area should be prepared just as conscientiously as the ramp itself. This must be very soft especially for the later overhead jumps. You can do this by jabbing and loosening the surface with a shovel or a pickaxe if there is not enough powder snow around. The landing area should be reworked frequently between jumps.

Skier: Gerhard Blöchl
Photo: Armin Blöchl
Location: Peiting

Water Ramps in Europe

There are several water ramps in the States, Canada and in Europe. Here is a list of a few of the biggest facilities that have a variety of big ramps and trampolines:

USA: Lake Placid, NY
Park City, UT
Steamboat Springs, CO

CAN: Quebec City, Quebec
Whistler Blackcomb, BC

EUR: Peiting im Schongau (GER)
Mettmenstetten (CH)
Wien Kaisermöhlendamm (AUT)
Tignes (FRA)

Ales Valenta Kicker in Stity (CZ)
Villach (AUT)
Eindhoven (NED)

You can find detailed information about them on the Internet. Most places provide camping facilities nearby in the summer, so you can spend a casual time there. For the water jumps, you need a helmet, a life jacket and old skis fitted with safety ropes.

Christoph Stark, Grischa Weber and Gerhard Blöchl. Photo: Armin Blöchl. Location: Peiting

2.5 Warming Up

The media hardly ever show an athlete warming up before performing a trendy sport. Is that because it is simply unnecessary, uncool or just wrong?

Of course, jumps are nothing like rhythmic gymnastics, but you still should not jump without a brief warm-up and stretch. Like a motorbike or a car, you can't expect a great performance straight after starting the engine in the morning. Give your body time to get slowly into gear.

Only after a little basic workout is it possible to demand a high level of coordination from your muscles and central nervous system. It will also speed up the learning process considerably and automatically protects you from unnecessary injuries. It is ill advised to take another jump when you are frozen stiff or exhausted, this is when you put yourself at most risk for an injury.

Here are some possible ways to warm up in the morning:

If you are warming up by yourself, you can jog or jump in place or do short sprints uphill. Make sure you don't forget your trunk muscles and your upper body, including your shoulder muscles. The easiest way to do this is by rotating your trunk and circling your arms.

In a group, it is possible to warm up with games like soccer, wrestling or snowball fights. These are fun to do and also raise your body temperature to the right level.

A common and very useful warm-up is chopping the jump landing with a shovel. We call this double injury prevention: firstly you ensure a safe landing area and secondly all that shoveling automatically warms you up, particularly the trunk, shoulders and arms. We also advise you to do a couple of takeoffs to finish the warm-up.

Don't stretch for too long before you jump, as it can be counterproductive. Do stretch your muscles briefly though, especially the front and back of your thighs, your calves and the inside of your thighs. Then do the same thing with the trunk, shoulder and neck muscles. Some jumpers also use this time for mental preparation by going through all the jumps they are going to do in their heads. Experience shows that it helps to always follow the same sequence in your warm-up. A morning routine and a familiar rhythm right at the start of a day's skiing give you a feeling of security. Especially in sports like this in which the mental side plays a key role, this security is an important first step in the right direction.

Never throw your own principles overboard; it is not a question of proving something to other people. Basically, you should only jump when you feel ready for it.

2.6 Mental Preparation

It goes without saying that we believe that you are all brave skiers. However, everyone must deal with his or her own personal fears. This creates its own special stimulus, for we first deliberately confront the risk and then get a rush of happiness if we manage the risk and complete the task successfully.

The oppressive feeling of anxiety you feel before new jumps is caused by the fear of the unknown or bad experiences during previous jumps. That is why the goal of every jumper must be to transform the negative anxiety that can hinder progress and even lead to injury into positive anxiety. By this we mean a healthy respect that protects you from overestimating yourself.

You can also control your mind if you keep to the above-mentioned learning principles and move toward your goal in small stages. It is not a weakness to sometimes take a step backward and try to improve the basics again. You should never feel forced to jump because of peer pressure or other external pressures.

You don't need to be too afraid of falling either, as this is just part of the learning process. Falling displays effort, so learn from your mistakes and work toward a better performance. Every attempt will teach you a lesson if you are sensitive enough to listen. Chapter 10 of this book deals with the right way to fall in more detail.

3 INSTRUCTIONS FOR LEARNING THE JUMPS

Most of this book is dedicated to showing you how to jump and ski safely. The jumps are presented in the form of photo sequences on snow; they are broken down to help the reader understand body position, vision, balance, and awareness at each point of the trick. Each image is accompanied by a detailed description of the movement it portrays. This procedure provides you with a methodical way of learning each jump.

This book is innovative in the way it presents the jumps in both the final form on the snow and during the early stages on the water or the trampoline. Some individual photos show the whole sequence of the jump in a way that is easy to understand visually.

From the first glance, the direction of the movement is clearly identifiable. The accompanying descriptions are deliberately kept brief and reduced to the essentials. We will describe the body's movement, balance, vision, static and dynamic positions. It should be understood that there are many ways to do each trick correctly. I urge you to explore your own capabilities and find the style and method that best suits you.

The combination of text and image is a prerequisite for understanding a sport's movement and, by providing a basic movement idea, enables focused learning. Concentrate on looking at the individual sequences and reading the text.

Pick up the book, irrespective of your ability, and you will have a quick look to refresh your memory of the most important movement elements and tips on the most common mistakes before you practice your jumps.

4 THE STRAIGHT JUMP

The Straight Jump, also known as the T-Set, is a basic component of every jump that can be done on the snow. Though this jump is simple, it is one of the most difficult to master. This jump helps to develop body awareness, control, balance, and stability in all phases of the jumping process. Mastery of it will help in the development of any aerial maneuver.

Many beginners, often motivated by videos and advertising images, try to do other more difficult jumps without first being able to master a controlled Straight Jump.

Of course, it looks more stylish if you immediately try to do a casual grab. We strongly recommend learning a Straight Jump first. Developing a strong foundation with the entrance, takeoff, flight and landing phases are very important. Basic gaps at this stage lead to learning blocks later on and, in the worst case, to injury.

Before embarking on jumps like flips and spins, you must be very secure performing Straight Jumps off both small and large jumps. Your Straight Jumps should be 100% controlled, so that you can learn different maneuvers more quickly later.

Even as you get more advanced, every jump session on the snow should start with Straight Jumps for height and distance to give you a feeling for flight and timing. This preparation allows even an experienced jumper to check the conditions of the jump and the landing area by getting feedback during the first Straight Jumps at maximum and minimum speeds, before he starts doing complex overhead jumps.

If you ever come across a New Schooler in the park who starts his day with a difficult trick, he is either very experienced or has already jumped from the ramp before. Otherwise, he is running a high and unnecessary risk.

Now we can finally start to look at the practical side, which is divided into four stages:

Phase 1: Approach
(the same for straight and spinning jumps)

Approaching the jump, the skier should have their balance over the balls of their feet with a slight pressure on their shins to maintain an athletic stance. The knees should be driven straight down the hill with shoulders stacked tall over the knees and feet. The knee and hip angles can be increased or decreased to initiate more or less lift when leaving the jump.

Phase 2: A slight bend at the hip and knee is all that is needed to begin. As the skier approaches the jump, his eyes should maintain a soft focus on the takeoff point. As the skier moves through the transition or belly (area where the angle of the jump increases leading to the takeoff point) of the jump, the legs should start resisting the increased pressure created by the increased angle. Approaching this position, the skier's eyes should now be lifting up, looking out past the end of the jump. With the upper body driving slightly forward to resist the jump's pressure, the lower body should begin to stand against the jump, finishing this movement by the takeoff point of the jump. At the takeoff point, the athlete's head, chest, hips, and knees should now be over the balls of the feet, with hands slightly in front of the body, about armpit height, and slightly out to the sides. This is the takeoff position.

Important: Phase two is where most tricks are either won or lost. If you have a good takeoff, you give yourself the best chance to perform the desired trick correctly. It is true that you can perform almost any trick with a poor takeoff, but you increase your chances of landing consistently with a good takeoff.

Phase 3: Air Time

Once the takeoff position has been completed, the body will begin to travel into the air toward its apex. The apex is the position at which the body reaches its maximum height and begins to descend. As the skier climbs into the air, he can begin to outstretch his arms slightly in front and out to each side. When using the arms to assist in balance and stability, the body should form what looks like the letter T in the air when viewed from the front. The head should be facing forward and tall. The athlete should resist the temptation to stare at the landing as it can lead to dropping your head and chest into the landing, taking your body out of balance. To assist in maintaining balance while in this position, it is recommended that the skier keeps the shoulders slightly forward, hollowing the chest. This position gives the athlete greater balance and stability when in flight and lessens the chance that the shoulders will slide behind the ball of the foot during landing.

Phase 4: Landing

As the athlete begins to descend back toward earth, it is important that he not only sees his landing but also down the hill in the direction he is traveling. By keeping your eyes up and looking down the fall line, it will allow you to carry over any small inconsistencies in the landing. Approaching the landing with a tall bodyline allows the athlete to absorb the landing with the least amount of impact. Depending on the landing conditions, the athlete will want to land on the balls of his feet with his shins driving forward into the fronts of his ski boots. With hands in front and a tall chest, the skier will be ready to take on the impact of the landing. When trying to quickly get back into a skiing rhythm, it is important to have good sight coming out of the jump.

Skier: Gerhard Blöchl
Photo: Armin Blöchl
Location: Zermatt

Methodical Aids:

It is possible to start learning the Straight Jump right away on the snow. However, it can also be simulated perfectly on the grass, a trampoline or on a diving board into a swimming pool. These simulation jumps are a great way to give you your first taste of the sensation of flying. An important advantage of simulating the jump is that the exercise is made easier, since you don't have to use a ski lift after every jump or rebuild the jump.

5 GRABS

Skier: Gerhard Blöchl
Photo: Martin Trautmann
Location: Zugspitze

Grabs are maneuvers that can be combined with nearly every jump. They consist of grabbing the ski during a jump and holding it firmly. This action enables a certain position to be frozen in the air for a while.

The longer a grab is held for, the more stylish it is. Every jumper develops his own style over time. It is not our role to judge which style is cool right now.

As previously mentioned, this book tries to provide the building blocks for those skiers who are interested. They can pick out the elements that are important to them and then find and express their own style by combining the basic jumps in this book with their own creative ideas.

For this reason, it is not possible for this book to focus on the jumps that are currently in style. You can find information about those jumps in Freeski magazines and films.

Beginners and novices should now be able combine the Straight Jump they have already practiced with various grabs before they progress to spins and flips. Using our photo sequences as an aid, you can quickly learn New School jumps for use in the terrain park.

Below, we list some of the grabs that have been most frequently performed in the past ten years. Of course, there will probably be many additional innovations and developments in the years to come.

Putting It All Into Practice

The approach, takeoff and landing for a grab maneuver are identical to that of the Straight Jump. However, a grab is now incorporated into the flight phase of the jump. When performing a grab, as in the Straight Jump, you should keep looking straight ahead throughout the jump.

5.1 Tail Grab

In the Tail Grab, the hand grips the inside of the ski. The legs are bent and the other arm is stretched out forward or to the side. By tweaking, the skier crosses his skis, which gives the jump its characteristic appearance. Structured presentation of the flight phase occurs in three parts:

Part 1:

The first part of the flight phase is performed like the Straight Jump to maintain stability in the air.

Part 2:

Then the knees are bent at right angles while the hips remain straight. At the same time, the right hand grips the inside of the right ski and the left arm is stretched out to stabilize the body (this can obviously also be done on the opposite side of the body). You then tweak, which pushes your body outward and makes your skis cross.

Part 3:

When you come out of this position, make sure that your arms and legs return simultaneously to the Straight Jump position so that you don't lose balance. The landing is then performed the same as in the Straight Jump.

Skier: Grischa Weber
Photo: Armin Blöchl
Location: Kitzsteinhorn

5.2 Mute Grab

In the Mute Grab, one hand grips the toe piece of the front ski binding. A characteristic of the jump is again the cross ski position, but in the Mute Grab, the grip is at the front. This position can then be frozen in the air. Structured presentation of the flight phase happens in three parts: Parts 1 and 3 are the same as the Tail Grab.

Part 1:

See the Tail Grab (p. 36).

Part 2:

Now sit on your heels and grip the outside of your left ski with your right hand in front of the toe piece. Then pull the ski to the right with your right hand while you extend your hips. At the same time, the left arm stabilizes the body by stretching out to the side. The hips can be arched, which is typical in a Back Flip combined with a Mute Grab. How you choose to perform it depends on your individual style. The jump can be done on the opposite side of the body.

Part 3:

See the Tail Grab (p. 36).

Skier: Gerhard Blöchl
Photo: Armin Blöchl
Location: Zugspitze

5.3 Japan Air

In the Japan Air, your skis are parallel while one hand grips the back of the rear ski binding. The jump resembles an Asian martial arts kick.

Here is a structured breakdown of the flight phase in three parts: Parts 1 and 3 are the same as for the Tail Grab and can be found in Chapter 5.1.

Part 1:

See Chapter 5.1.

Part 2:

While the right leg remains straight, tuck up your left leg. Then your right hand grips the inside of the left ski underneath the back of the rear binding.

For this grip to be possible your hips must be tilted slightly sideways. At the same time, your left arm is stretched out and up to the side to provide stability. Make sure that your skis are parallel throughout.

Part 3:

See Chapter 5.1.

Skier: Gerhard Blöchl
Photo: Armin Blöchl
Location: Zugspitze

5.4 Safety Grab

The Safety Grab is the simplest of all the Grab variations and is therefore easy to incorporate into more complex jumps.

Your legs are tucked up, and you hold the center of the skis. Here is a structured breakdown of the flight phase into three parts: Parts 1 and 3 are the same as for the Tail Grab and can be found in Chapter 5.1.

Part 1:

See Chapter 5.1.

Part 2:

Tuck up both legs and grip the center of the right ski along the outside edge. At the same time, raise your left arm to the side.

The skis should remain parallel and either hip-width apart or together, depending on your individual style.

Part 3:

See Chapter 5.1.

Skier: Sven Küenle Photo: k2sports.net Location: Zugspitze (Safety Grab in an overhead jump)

6 SPINS

A spin should be part of the repertoire of every good skier, whether he is a ski instructor, racer or Freeskier. This jump is even described in detail in the syllabus of the Swiss ski instructors' training course. Over the past few years, several variations of these jumps have sprung up. The most photographed version was the 360° Mute Grab, as performed by American Jonny Moseley in front of an unbelievably large crowd at the Nagano Olympics in 1998.

Below is an explanation of how easy it is to learn a few variations of the Spin. We start with the 180°, then move on to the 360° and finish with multiple turns. Before attempting an Off-Axis Spin or Spins with Grabs, you should first master the normal, extended 360°, also known as a helicopter.

Before we introduce the 180°, we would like to go into a little more detail about skiing backward. With Spins, as with many other jumps, it is possible to perform a backwards takeoff or landing. As switch takeoffs and landings are not exactly easy, it is important to study the following description of Fakie skiing thoroughly.

Fakie Skiing

Before you jump or land fakie from a kicker, it is absolutely essential that you feel safe skiing backward on the slopes. To begin with, you should try skiing backwards on a very gentle slope. This start will allow you to avoid building up too much speed and then falling because you have lost control.

At very low speeds, you can manage to slide or spin from the forward skiing position to skiing backward. When skiing backwards, make sure that your feet are parallel. If your speed is too high, you can brake in the plow position by pointing your ski

Skier: Mike Morse
Photo: Patrick Reeves

tails together. When you slide back into the forward skiing position, your feet should remain parallel. You should slide or spin in the same direction of rotation in which you slid into the backward skiing movement.

Don't think too much about which direction you should turn though! You will usually find that you automatically turn in the right direction. The use of twintip skis may provide better control while skiing backwards, but are not necessary on well-groomed slopes.

Most people find it easier to turn to the left. **TIP**

It is obviously not sufficient just to slide backward. That is why we have given you a few tips on how to carve backward without crashing, the most important of which is to keep your feet parallel. You will notice that you automatically curve to the right if you look backward over your left shoulder, and vice versa if you look over your right shoulder. For very experienced skiers, it will be possible to ski sharp turns backward.

But how can you ski backward looking behind you without making a curve? This ability will be important later when you slide onto a jump in the fakie position. To maintain a straight direction, you must steer with your hips and shoulders in the opposite direction to which your head is turned. Flatter slopes will become more interesting as they are great for practicing this exercise. Only when you have mastered fakie skiing on the slopes should you attempt to do it on a jump.

6.1 The 180°

To learn the basics of a 180°, you don't need to build a jump. You can try the 180° off the ridges in the snow and jump directly from skiing forward into skiing backward. However, it is more sensible to use a gentle, low ramp until you start to build consistency.

There are four phases to the 180°:

Phase 1:   Approach

(See Chapter 4 "Straight Jump")

Phase 2:   Takeoff

With a strong stance, the athlete begins to resist the pressure on the jump, straightening the body at the end of the jump. At this point, the movements of the upper and lower body separate slightly. The lower body finishes the takeoff with an explosive extension of the hips and knees in the same manner as the T-set. With the skis tracking straight off the jump, the hips line up over the knees and the balls of the feet making a perpendicular angle to flat ground (NOT the Jump). At this point, the upper body should begin a slight rotation in the direction that it wants to spin led by even shoulders and head. The eyes should be looking forward with the head held upright.

Phase 3:   Flight phase

You should keep your body tensed and extended in the air. Hold your arms slightly in front of your body. Control your spin by bringing your arms in toward your side to speed up the rotation, extend them away from your side to slow it down. During the rotation, your head should remain in a neutral position, so don't look down at the ground! Look at the ground using your peripheral vision.

Phase 4:   Landing

Your field of vision on landing is naturally reduced when moving backward. You mainly see the landing area behind you and to the side, so make sure that it is spacious with no obstacles in the way. Your legs must definitely be kept parallel and hip-width apart. Once you have landed the jump, you can either continue fakie or spin around back to normal position.

Of course, it is also possible to start and land the 180° fakie forward. Many people will find this easier. The great difficulty lies in hitting a clean takeoff. If you then choose not to turn because you are afraid of missing the takeoff, this is not a problem as you can always land backward.

In general, the 180° jump is very difficult off very big ramps, as very few people are patient enough to rotate slowly without losing tension.

6.2 The 360°

With the 180° under your belt, it will surely not be too hard for you to learn the 360°. Before you practice the basic movements of this jump, it is important to emphasize that the higher rotational speed around the vertical axis required by this jump increases the risk of injury. So before attempting the 360° on skis in the snow, you should have already rehearsed the movement, e.g. from a diving board in the pool or on a mini-trampoline.

Methodical Introduction

This time, we are going to prepare for the jump from the 3ft diving board in the swimming pool, though the preparation is the same as on a mini-trampoline. The takeoff from the board is two-footed. You don't need to start with an approach run. In the Straight Jump, the takeoff direction is forward and upward. The momentum during the takeoff initiates the rotation around the vertical axis. Turning the head, shoulders and hips in the desired direction during the extension creates this rotation. As you start to rotate, stretch out your arms to provide additional stability. Bringing your arms toward your body will increase the speed of rotation if you are spinning too slowly. It is possible to slow the rotation by stretching your arms away from your body. The most common error during execution is to look at the ground during the rotation phase to spot your landing zone. This action automatically leads to a diagonal body position in the air, which compromises jump stability.

After your first 360°s have gone well, it is important that you now experiment in the water. You should start to develop air awareness and begin to improve the quality of the movement. You may slowly incorporate multiple rotations or grabs into the jump as your proficiency increases.

Skier: David Babic
Photo: Patrick Reeves

Skier: David Babic
Photo: Patrick Reeves

Movement Description of the 360° with Skis

Phase 1: Approach

(See Chapter 4 "Straight Jump") pg. 31

Phase 2: Takeoff

With a strong stance, the athlete begins to resist the pressure on the jump, straightening the body at the end of the jump. At this point the movements of the upper and lower body separate slightly. The lower body finishes the takeoff in the same manner as the T-set. With the skis tracking straight off the jump, the hips line up over the knees and the balls of the feet make a *perpendicular angle* to *flat ground* (NOT the Jump). At this point, the upper body should begin a slight rotation in the direction that it wants to spin led by even shoulders and head. To perform a 360° spin, the rotation should be significantly stronger than for the 180°. As with the 180°, your eyes should be looking forward with the head held upright.

Phase 3: Flight

As the athlete lifts-off the jump the skis should continue to track straight but begin to rotate from the shoulder's initiation. The shoulders should continue to evenly rotate in the same position. The head and vision can now leave the forward position to find a natural, even position between the shoulders. Keeping the head square and the eyes looking straight ahead helps to keep your body in alignment while in the air. Once the upper body has moved through the first quarter of the rotation, it is time for the lower body to catch up. Simply squeezing the stomach muscles allows the lower body to catch up so that the all body parts are together moving as one. The athlete can adjust the rotation speed by making their body bigger or smaller. Outstretched arms will help to slow the spin, while pulling in the arms close to the body will speed up the movement. With practice, the athlete will begin to develop proficiency with maintaining a good rotational velocity.

Phase 4: Landing

When the athlete has reached 3/4 of his rotation he can begin to prepare for the landing. Some athletes like to look down slightly to spot their landing as they approach the ground. However, keeping your vision up as much as possible will help to enable a stable four-point landing. During the landing, you will be carrying some momentum, so slow down enough that you do not spin through the landing. Upon landing, quickly scan your eyes up and look down the fall line to see what is ahead.

A good tip is to pull the tips of your toes toward you to avoid turning like a banana.

Maintaining good vision can be made easier by having a friend stand behind the jump. Once in the air, try to spot out your friend while backwards. Just make eye contact and continue on with your rotation.

Common Problems

Throwing the trick early: In an attempt to finish the trick sooner, people tend to try to start the trick earlier. This action causes many problems; lost balance on takeoff, lost equipment during takeoff, stalled rotation, landing on side. To remedy this problem, try thinking of the 360° as happening 3 to 4 feet out in front of the jump. Doing the trick away from the jump will help to develop patience during takeoff.

Unintentional off-axis air: This problem results from an unbalanced takeoff or failure to make the proper adjustment while in the air. Many times this problem can be fixed by simply adjusting your vision. Try raising your vision throughout the trick, as looking down can dramatically affect your balance. The problem can also develop from an imbalance in your feet, hips, shoulders, or arms. Try a more balanced takeoff with even shoulders and maintaining equal pressure through both feet on takeoff.

6.3 The 540° and 720°

When you have mastered the 360°, you can move on to experiment with multiple rotations. In order to spin additional rotations, you will need either more air or more twist in the upper body during takeoff.

These changes can be executed in the same manner as when you increased from 180° to 360°. To minimize the risk of injury, make your first attempts in a pool or on a mini trampoline before jumping with skis in the snow.

Skier: Margerita Marbler (AUT)
Photo: Blizzard

Multiple Mogul World Cup Champion
World Cup Champion Dual 2002/2003
3rd Place Overall World Cup 2003/2004
10th Place Olympic Games Salt Lake City
2002
3rd Place World Championships 2005
More information at www.marbler.com

Skier: Margerita Marbler
Photo: Armin Blöchl
Location: Zermatt

Skier: Gerhard Blöchl
Photo: Armin Blöchl
Location: Kitzsteinhorn

7 FLIPS

Back flips or *front flips* represent a great dream for many skiers. Who would not like to say that they could do flips on skis? This dream is easier to realize than you may think. For many people, flips are even easier to learn than the helicopter. Our methodical approach makes it possible for every skier to do a back flip in powder snow. On the right terrain, back flips or front flips are fantastic show jumps. Admiration and respect will soon follow your first flips!

The first flips on skis were captured on film back in 1907. Today, overhead jumps are featured in almost every trendy or lifestyle sport. From wakeboarding to freestyle motorcross, the public appreciates those athletes who can perform such spectacular overhead jumps.

7.1 Front Flip

This jump is one of the basic overhead maneuvers. With the right height and distance, it can look really stylish. It is a good choice for the first overhead jump, as many of you will already have performed a similar movement either on the trampoline or from the diving board in the swimming pool.

The initial mental barrier is easier to overcome in the forward flip than in the backward flip. Eventually though, most jumpers will realize that the backward flip is actually easier than the forward flip. Halfway through the back flip the jumper can see the ground with time to adjust for the landing. However, it is psychologically easier to begin with the forward flip.

Methodical Approach to the Forward Flip

It is essential to learn the forward flip in a methodical way on the trampoline or on the diving board in a swimming pool before attempting it on skis. Only when you have really learned the basic movement well will you be able to transfer the jump to skis without a high risk of injury. Doing a forward roll on the floor, dive rolls, or jumping on a mini trampoline will also help with this learning process.

In our opinion, the forward flip is easiest to learn on a mini trampoline, which can be found in many gymnastic facilities. If you do not have access to a trampoline, it is also possible to practice the necessary movements from a diving board in the swimming pool. However, we will be illustrating how to perform the jumps on a mini trampoline. We recommend that you read the instructions for the mini trampoline in any case.

In the forward flip, anyone can see that because the element of rotation must always be around the latitudinal axis, the steps should be learned as a whole. It would be dangerous to start with half a rotation, as you could with the helicopter. To make learning easier, we can practice in the gym with a mini trampoline, a box and a mat.

These should be placed as follows: three boxes are placed so that two of them are lengthwise and the third is across. Lay a soft floor mat lengthwise over the boxes. Finally, place the mini trampoline in front of the crossways box. It is a good idea to put a second floor mat behind the structure, and also around the sides for safety reasons.

Learning Forward Rotation Around the Latitudinal Axis

To begin, familiarize yourself with the mini trampoline again by making a few tuck jumps from the box structure. If you have not been on a trampoline for a while, you should also do a few forward rolls on the floor. You can then immediately go on to do your dive roll from the mini trampoline onto the mat.

You should always perform a two-footed takeoff from the trampoline, simultaneously raising your arms forward and upward. In the case of the jump roll, you should land hands first on the mat, tuck your head, and then roll onto your back.

Jumper:
A pupil of
Armin Blöchl

After a few jump rolls, try just brushing the mat with your hands. Immediately after touching it, pull your arms toward your body and tuck your head into your chest. Pulling your arms rapidly toward your body while you roll up causes you to rotate around the latitudinal axis.

The next goal is to land on your upper back without using your hands at all. You can manage to do this with a more powerful takeoff and a more dynamic initiation to the rotation.

At this point, you will only have limited experience of rotation around the latitudinal axis. In order for you to eventually avoid landing on your back, you must increase the speed of rotation. Do this by rolling into a ball, which increases the speed of rotation allowing you to land sitting on your heels.

Important: When you roll into a ball, your knees must always be hip-width apart to prevent them from hitting your chin.

Learning the Landing in Isolation

In skiing, it is extremely important to learn the landing phase of the forward flip separately from the rotation stage in the learning process. For now, you should roll into a ball and lie on the floor with your chin on your chest and your hands wrapped around your shins. This is the position in which you will reach the highest rotational speed.

To slow down the speed of rotation, extend your hips quickly, kick your legs forward and raise your hands. You should simulate this action several times while lying on the floor so that your body learns the correct movement pattern and allows you to mentally visualize and simulate the landing action.

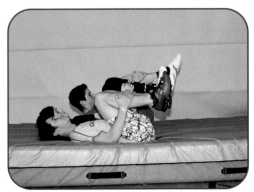 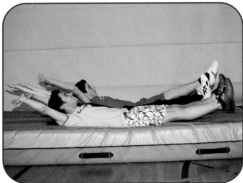

Pupils of Armin Blöchl

Now do the flip as before, except that you are about to land horizontally on your back on the mat. Try to straighten your hips and legs quickly so that you land on the mat with your body almost fully extended. As in the previous simulation, your hands are brought diagonally upward.

Combination of Rotation and Landing Preparation

Apparatus structure
Place a box at right angles to your approach direction, and put the mini trampoline in front of it, as before. Behind the box, place a mat lengthways on the floor. Then lay another mat diagonally on the first mat and the box. Place more mats at the ends and the sides for safety reasons.

As in the preparation exercises, perform the flip across the new structure. As soon as your back is horizontal above or touching the diagonal mat, extend your hips, legs and arms as you previously learned in isolation.

You may even land on your feet already. Repeat this stage as often as possible and practice so that the transfer becomes more controlled and the timing and spatial orientation of the opening up improve. Only then can you start to vary the approach speed and height of the jump.

Jumper: Pupil of Armin

Front Flip with Skis

If you use a water ramp, you should start by doing a few Straight Jumps to get the length of your approach right. Most water ramps have a very steep approach.

This steepness doesn't necessarily mean a high approach speed, as the friction from the plastic mats is quite high. Experienced jumpers often use the Front flip from the water ramp as a warm-up or fun jump.

On most water ramps, you stand perpendicular to the direction of the approach run to avoid slipping on the mat. Only after jumping, when you turn your skis through 90° do you achieve the correct starting position. This jump with a turn should be very solid. You can practice it on the grass on skis beforehand.

There is nothing worse than stumbling right at the start. During the approach, keep looking ahead past the jump with your head up. Bring your imaginary poles in front of your body, without letting your arms dangle. This stance brings your body into a central position.

You can feel the central body position when your weight is evenly distributed over the heels and balls of your feet and your shinbone rests on the tongue of your ski boots. Your hips and knees are slightly bent. For your landing to be as stable as possible, your feet should be hip-width apart and parallel.

Description of the Front Flip with Skis

In the first photo in the sequence, you can see how Gerhard stretches his arms forward and upward and takes off from the balls of his feet. You should be able to feel the tongue of your ski boots throughout. Keep looking forward and upward.

In the second photo, he leaves the kicker. His head is upright and he is looking forward across the landing area.

Then the shoulders are brought down to shoulder level with a powerful movement as you tuck your heels up (see photo 3).

Skier: Gerhard Blöchl
Photo: Armin Blöchl
Location: Peiting

The legs move upward and the body begins to rotate in an extended position. The head is upright throughout. Only when the highest point of the flight curve is reached and the heels are higher than the hips – as seen in photo 4 – do you roll your body up explosively. For this, bring the head toward the chest and tuck up your legs. Gripping your knees or shins with your hands helps you to hold the position better – see photos 5, 6 and 7 of the sequence.

As soon as your back is horizontal, release your hands from your legs and simultaneously extend the hips by explosively stretching your legs downward, as shown in photos 8 and 9. This stretch slows down the rotation. If you need to slow down even more to avoid over rotation, your arms can also be raised.

In your first attempts in the snow, it is a good idea to leave your legs slightly in front of your body (photo 10). This stance will give you a better chance of falling on to your back, until you perfect your timing. The worst thing that can happen is that you over rotate and land on your stomach.

This must be avoided at all costs. Photo 11 shows that, upon landing, you are still looking in the direction of movement and never directly at the landing area. You land with your body in a central position. Even when you land in water, you still need to land with body tension.

Transfer of the Forward Flip with Skis in the Snow

Here, we really recommend that you practice first on the water kicker. But if you have gained a good feeling for the movement on the mini trampoline or diving board, you can go on to perform it on the snow directly. Along with the other elements you have practiced for this jump, you also really need to have mastered the Straight Jump to avoid problems with the takeoff and landing.

For your first attempts, try to find a ramp that has a steep takeoff and landing slope. Chop the landing with care and make sure there is at least 3 feet of natural, loose powder snow. If necessary, fill the craters that are occasionally created by landing. Jumps where the takeoff angle is too flat are not suitable, as they don't provide enough heel lift to perform the trick properly.

Important Tips:

While your sense of timing is not yet sufficiently developed, it is better to land on your back than to over rotate. If you wear a back protector and the landing area is well prepared, it is preferable to land on your back than on your stomach.

Always remember to keep your mouth open, as a strong impact can cause excess pressure on the lungs that damages the bronchial tubes and can make you cough up blood.

Only use specifically designed protective gear when attempting new tricks in which crashes are more likely.

7.2 Back Flip

Skier: David Babic
Photo: Patrick Reeves

Whether you are a ski racer, a skiing instructor or a recreational skier, you have probably wondered if you will be able to do a back flip on skis. You can quickly put this dream into practice, for you only need to do a few preparation exercises for the back flip to become possible. Along with the front flip, it is one of the easier jumps to learn.

There are a few jumpers who will never be able to do a 360° but who are capable of excellent flips, and these days, no good free skier's repertoire can be without a back flip. Every good line in off-piste terrain looks even more fantastic when you add a simple back flip.

Along with the front flip and side flip, it forms the basis for all overhead jumps. The back flip is also a prerequisite for nearly all overhead jumps with spins. By combining it with your choice of grab, you can give the jump your own individual style.

In the initial stages, the back flip may seem more difficult than the front flip for some people. Later on, most people actually prefer to jump the back flip, though, as it is easier to control because the landing area is visible earlier.

Methodical Introduction to the Back Flip
To perform a back flip with skis, it is essential that you learn in a methodical way on a trampoline or on a diving board in a swimming pool. Only by acquiring good movement experience, can you transfer the jump to skis without a high risk of injury. You must first be able to do a backward roll on the floor and have some experience on a trampoline.

In our opinion, it is easier to learn the flip using a mini trampoline, which you can find in many gymnasiums. If you don't have access to a trampoline, it is also possible to acquire the necessary movement skills on a swimming pool diving board. In any case, here we show you the simpler way using a mini trampoline.

If you use a diving board, all the initial exercises are identical, and only later do the methods diverge. Even if this is the case, we still recommend that you read the procedure for the mini trampoline.

Like the front flip, the back flip rotation should move along the latitudinal axis at each stage of the flip. This means that this flip must also be learned as a whole. You cannot start with a half turn, as you do in the heli, for example. The jump is easier to learn if your friends can act as spotters for you, so that you can quickly get a feeling for the timing and spatial awareness.

Learning to Rotate Backward Around the Latitudinal Axis

The initial learning phase should involve going over the basic requirements, like the backward roll and possibly Straight Jumps on the mini trampoline or diving board. A flip-like movement can be simulated quite safely by doing a backward roll on a sloping surface.

A sloped surface can be created for this purpose, e.g., laying a thick padded mat at an angle on top of a box creates a diagonal plane from which to roll down. For safety reasons, make sure the area around the mat is padded and clear of any obstacles.

Backward Roll on a Sloping Surface

Lie on your back on the sloping surface, put your arms in the air behind your head and keep them there. By raising your legs quickly, you initiate the backward roll, and you end up sitting on your heels.

After starting with a very simple simulation, which already gives you a first movement, the next step is the wall flip.

Pupil of Armin Blöchl

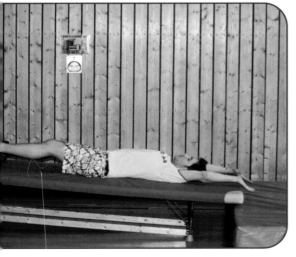

Wall Flip

The wall flip is an excellent exercise that prepares you for the back flip. The transfer of this methodical preparation exercise for the back flip is only possible in a group of three people. As you already know, this is not a team sport, but it is nearly impossible to learn there tricks without the support of friends. It is just as important to practice the sport with friends you can trust, who can act as spotters. Then the exercise can begin.

The person doing the exercise stands facing the wall and holds his arms out in front of him. We recommend that this exercise be done standing on a thin gym mat or on grass. The spotters stand to the right and left of the athlete gripping his or her arm or shirt, ready to assisting in the spot.

Pupil of Armin Blöchl. Spotters: Doris Huber/Armin Blöchl

Once the jumper is supported securely, he walks up the wall until his hips and legs are higher than his head. He then pushes off from the wall and simultaneously throws back his head and pulls his knees into his chest. As soon as he can see the floor, he immediately extends his hips and legs again so that his body is almost straight when he lands.

Especially at the beginning, it is important that the spotters bring the jumper to a stable position. To avoid falling over, the spotters must stand with their shoulders as close as possible to the jumper. They also must stand securely so that they don't let themselves get pushed away from the wall.

An Alternative to the Wall Flip

"Throw Flip"

If you cannot find a suitable wall, it is possible to do a similar exercise without a wall, although you do need a group of four. The flip jumper sits on the hands of a spotter who is sitting on the floor with his legs apart. Two other helpers stand to his left and right and grip the jumper's upper arms as they did for the wall flip. The jumper then takes off and the spotters help him to turn backwards.

For this to work, you have to act as a team. The two spotters at the side help the jumper until he is standing safely on his feet again.

Pupil of Armin Blöchl

Back Flip on the Mini Trampoline

For this method, place the mini trampoline with the lower side next to the edge of a landing mat.

The jumper then stands with his back to the mat on the trampoline. The two spotters stand on either side of him beside the trampoline, with one foot on the landing mat. The spotter to the left grips the jumper's shirt with his right hand, and with his left hand he supports the rotation at the back of the nearest thigh. As soon as the jumper is stable, he makes two little bounces on the trampoline and on the third bounce he takes off from both feet. It is possible to support this movement by swinging his arms forward and upward.

The flip is initiated with a strong lifting motion by the entire body, driving the feet and center of mass toward the sky. To increase rotation in the flip, one should tuck up his legs quickly while keeping the head neutral. This rotation can be made easier by grabbing the back of the knees. Finally, when the jumper can see the ground, he they can begin to come out of the tuck position, straighten his legs and open out his hips.

Jumper: Pupil of Armin Blöchl. Spotters: Doris Huber/Armin Blöchl

It is a good idea for the jumper to count to three out loud so that the spotters know exactly when he is going to jump. As the jumper gradually gets a better feeling for the timing and spatial awareness of the jump, the spotters' role becomes less and less important, until they eventually just help to push the jumper's lower back and thighs, and then finally the jump can be performed alone. **TIP**

Jumper: pupil of Armin Blöchl. Spotters: Doris Huber/Armin Blöchl

Alternative: Back Flip from 3ft. Diving Board

After gaining a feeling for the movement with a few simulation exercises, so the body experiences the movement in rough form, you can now try to do the back flip into water. This is not usually dangerous from the 3ft. board, provided, of course, that you can swim!

Stand at the very end of the board with your back to the water, so that your heels are hanging over the end of the board. Look straight ahead, with your arms slightly bent by your sides, then lean backward slightly in this position. Leaning back will allow the athlete to flip away from the end of the board, protecting him from injury. Once momentum has been generated toward the water, the takeoff can begin by swinging your arms forward and upward.

The flip is initiated with a strong lifting motion by the entire body, driving the feet and center of mass toward the sky. To increase rotation in the flip, one should tuck up his legs by pulling them in quickly toward the chest (not vice versa), while keeping the head neutral. This is known as the **pull position** and can be made easier by grabbing the back of the knees. Finally, when the jumper can see the ground he can begin to come out of the tuck by straightening the legs and hips.

Skier: Gerhard Blöchl
Photo: Armin Blöchl
Location: Peiting

Back Flip with Skis

You can read some basic information about water ramps and a detailed description of the approach in Chapter 7.1, "Front Flips with Skis."

Movement Description of the "Tucked Back Flip with Skis"

Phase 1. Entrance

This position is similar to a straight jump. The athlete should approach the jump in the same manner, except that he should stand a bit taller, with less weight driving on the shins. As the athlete moves through the transition of the jump, the body should move in a *perpendicular angle* to the curve of the jump. In performing this movement, pressure will leave the front of the ski boot and weight will transfer to the heel. The athlete's vision should initially be focused on the end of the jump but approaching the transition should move out past the jump.

Phase 2. Takeoff

As the athlete reaches the end of the jump, the body should be moving *perpendicular* to the *curve* of the jump. Flip rotation can be initiated from the shoulders and or feet, but probably the most consistent method is to lift the trick from your center-of-mass (COM). Some athletes try to focus on lifting their belly button to the sky. Projecting your COM into the air gives you height and control of the flip. This lifting method prevents the tendency to sling the trick. A strong core will bring the feet with the rest of the body so that all body parts are flipping together as one. A slight arm movement can assist in the takeoff. If used, I would recommend keeping the arm swing similar to the T-set movement. It is important to keep your vision looking forward, past the jump and down the hill on takeoff. The head should be balanced over the shoulders and the rest of the body.

Common Mistakes:

1. Leading the flip with your head. Causes the rest of your body to be left behind, stall out, or even sling by landings. To fix: try to keep your head forward longer and focus on flipping from your belly button. Also, if stalling out is a problem, try driving your feet more on takeoff.
2. Slinging. Caused by being overambitious in an attempt to land fuzzy side up! Results in over rotation, with a tendency to result in a sore back and neck. To fix: focus on lifting the trick higher into the air. Another remedy is to try to spot your skis or toes throughout the first half of the trick.
3. Sucking up the takeoff. A fear of amplitude and commitment can result in low Unidentified Flying Objects (UFO's), which in turn results in many short crashed landings. This result is caused by a soft takeoff, usually in the hips and knees, at the takeoff point of the jump. To fix: simply stand stronger against the jump and allow yourself to carry higher into the air.

Phase 3. Trick

With your whole body lifting off the jump, your vision can stay forward or simply move with your head as it begins to flip backwards. At this point, you should start asking yourself: How fast am I flipping? How big am I? How must I adjust to land on my feet? To answer these questions, you will need to gain air sense. To do this, practice, practice, practice! To speed up your flip, simply shorten your body by bringing your knees closer to your chest, not the other way around! To slow down your flip, elongate you body with your hands stretched out above your head. You can use any variety and magnitude of these positions to control the flip.

Phase 4. Landing

Once you have reached the inverted position (upside down), you should be able to spot the ground below. Depending on your flip speed and height, you can adjust your foot position to maximize your landing potential. As with all flips, you will be carrying some momentum that will need to be handled when landing. To adjust for this momentum, land with your feet slightly behind where you would for a straight jump. This adjustment will allow you to handle the momentum of the flip, making for a clean exit.

Common Problems:

1. Flipping to your back. Many times people do not adjust their flip speed and height, resulting in inconsistent landings. To fix: work on raising the flip higher into the air instead of farther down the hill. Also, adjusting when you see the ground (pulling or stretching) will help you find your feet more often.
2. Reaching for the landing. It was right there! This problem happens when people are anxious to get their feet back on the ground. Just be patient. Let your momentum bring your feet around to the landing. Pulling your feet in for the landing is easier than stretching at the last minute.
3. Head down on landing. Staring at your landing causes people to miss the terrain that is ahead. See your landing, but allow your vision to work down the hill. Doing so will allow you to carry over any difficult landings and prepare you for what is ahead.

If you sometimes land on your back in the water, it is not dangerous as long as you keep your mouth open. If you should happen to land on your stomach, which in a simple back flip will almost never happen, tuck up your arms and legs and make a cannonball. We would like to tell those who already know how hard water can be that the surface tension of the water can be greatly reduced by aiming a jet of water from a simple hose at the landing point.

Enjoy practicing!

Transferring the Back flip with Skis onto the Snow

Don't try the back flip on the snow until you have sufficient experience on the water jump. For sports psychological reasons, the danger of refusal is very high, regardless of how good the flip works on the trampoline or the diving board. After extended practice, the tuck part of the jump is reduced more and more until it becomes a straight layout back flip. The hips must be pressed forward even more strongly and the shins actively pushed upward so that you have enough rotation around the latitudinal axis.

If you want to combine the back flip with various grabs later, you should know at this point that grabs affect the rotation speed. The Mute Grab has a similar effect, as the tuck position, i.e., rotation, is accelerated. With the Japan Air and the Tail Grab, there is always a risk of twisting. You should therefore, first stabilize the basic jump and then slowly experiment.

A steep and well-prepared landing slope is extremely important for all overhead jumps. Steep landings will disperse more of the impact force over a greater distance, as the athlete will be landing with gravity instead of against it. **TIP**

7.3 Side Flip

Skier: David Babic
Photo: Patrick Reeves

The side flip is the third basic overhead jump, and it is characterized by a rotation around the vertical axis. Many people consider it to be a rather unusual jump, as the side flip is quite rare in most sports compared to the front or back flip. A clear advantage of the side flip is that one can see the landing area during the whole rotation.

However, it can't be classified as easier or more difficult when compared with the other two basic jumps.

Methodical Introduction to the Side Flip

The side flip should also be learned on the mini trampoline or the 3ft. diving board, so that the rotation around the vertical axis can be executed correctly. The only previous experience you need is the humble cartwheel. Repeating this action many times gives you the experience of rotating around the vertical axis.

Learning the Sideways Rotation Around the Vertical Axis

The side flip is easiest to learn on the mini trampoline. It is also possible to learn it on the 3ft. diving board, but there you must do without the help of a spotter. For the apparatus structure in the gym, place a soft landing mat beside the lower side of the trampoline. You can best get the necessary kinesthetic idea of the side flip by doing the following exercises: You will already have discovered which is your preferred side to turn around the vertical axis by practicing the cartwheel. Here we describe the side flip to the left. Stand on the trampoline sideways to the direction of movement, with your feet hip-width apart. After the third bounce, dynamically pull up both legs to the right to form a tuck position, supported by pulling your right arm upward. Bend your hips and head actively to the left. It is easiest if you try to grip your thigh explosively with your left hand. Throughout the rotation, look straight ahead at a fixed point so that you don't twist in the air. To start with, the spotter stands behind the jumper and pushes the jumper's hips around as he turns. The spotter should make sure that he crosses his left arm over his right in preparation of this support, prior to the jump. The spotter's function becomes more and more passive until he is just there to provide stability and then finally the jumper can do the flip by himself.

Athlete: David Babic. Photographer: Dan Starke. Location: Park City, UT.

Side Flips with Skis

You will find basic information about water ramps and a detailed description of the approach in Chapter 7.1, "Front Flips with Skis."

Skier: Gerhard Blöchl
Photo: Armin Blöchl
Location: Peiting

Movement Description of the Side Flip with Skis
The Loop

Phase 1. Entrance

See T-Set Phase 1.

Phase 2. Takeoff

As you begin to rise up toward the end of the jump, you will begin to stand up tall with your hips and knees. The big difference with this trick is that you will want to initiate the side flip at the liftoff point of the jump. When flipping to the right, you will lift your left arm and shoulder toward the sky. At the same time, you will want to side bend to your right, dropping your right arm and shoulder toward the side of your right knees. With your lower body still balanced over both feet, you should continue to track straight off the jump until you are completely in the air. You vision should be up, looking out past the jump and should start to rotate as the shoulders bend to the side.

Phase 3. Trick

As your skis leave the jump, they should begin a vertical climb to a horizontal position as your upper body continues to drop to the side. Your eyes can stay forward, spotting a point directly in front of you. In some cases, if your take off leans slightly back, you may lose sight of the ground for an instant. Once you reach an inverted position (skis directly above head), you should begin to recognize your flip speed and amplitude. At this point, you can make adjustments to help you prepare for your landing. Adjusting your flip speed is similar to the back flip; pull your knees to your chest to speed up, straighten your body to slow it down. It takes a while to learn the correct adjustment technique but is worth spending some time learning.

Phase 4. Landing

As your body passes the inverted position, you should be able to spot your landing. Allowing yourself to adjust for the momentum of your flip will help you bring this trick to your feet. If your body is flipping fast, leave your feet slightly behind in the rotation as they will slide into the landing position from the momentum of the flip. When you spot your landing, try to place your feet back under your body so that you land in the stacked position, with the balls of your feet in alignment with your hips and shoulders. On landing, your vision should be up, looking down the fall line.

Transfer of the Side Flip with Skis to the Snow

Once you have practiced sufficiently, you can try the jump on the snow. Of course, we recommend, as with all overhead maneuvers, that the landing area is very well prepared. It is possible to combine the side flip with various grabs. Make sure you can master the basic jump safely first though!

Your vision is key to hitting this trick correctly. One way to practice proper vision is to perform cartwheels on the ground while staring at a point in front of you. This practice will help you get in the habit of looking forward while your body rotates through the loop. During the jump, make sure that you takeoff cleanly, forward and upward and only turn sideways off the ramp at the last moment.

 TIP

8 FLIPS WITH SPIN

Any combination of flipping and spinning creates some of the most complex movements in sports. In Chapter 7, we described a methodical way of learning the three basic overhead jumps that you can practice with friends. The jumps below, presented by the authors with brief movement descriptions, are only to be practiced under direct professional supervision. It is best to look for a trampoline, gymnastics or diving coach. Personal experience has shown that only direct guidance with professional spotters can ensure that you learn quickly and, above all, safely.

A thorough and sports scientific explanation of the front and back corkscrew flips with different learning methods would easily fill a whole book, but it would be no substitute for expert personal guidance. Let it be known that there are many different ways to perform these tricks correctly. It is this book's attempt to show you the most stock method, in hopes that you will land fuzzy side up. It is up to you to get creative with your style and make the trick your own!

As in many other sports, multiple twist jumps around the longitudinal and latitudinal axes are developing very rapidly in new school sports. This kind of jump will be easiest to learn for those with a trampolining background. Many internationally successful New School professionals have been using a trampoline for years. An hour with a trampoline coach costs way less than a ski lift pass, and is extremely helpful.

Of course, we don't advise you against experimenting with the following jumps on the 3ft. diving board or using a water ramp, for there will always be athletes who can experiment by themselves with great success. You should know that the injury risk is significantly higher, though.

Skier: Luke Westerlund
Photo: Patrick Reeves

8.1 Misty

Skier: David Babic
Photo: Dan Starke
Location: Park City – UT

The Misty is classified as an Off-Axis trick. Characteristics of this jump are that the rotation is not purely around the longitudinal and latitudinal axes, as in gymnastics or aerials, but the jumps – as in snowboarding – are at an angle, which gives them their rather unique appearance. This can be best appreciated by watching the jump from the front or the back.

The easiest way to learn the Misty is basically as a front flip with a corkscrew, which you can learn with a trampoline coach. Changing to a Misty has the advantage of allowing you to see the landing area sooner than a straight front flip. This makes it a suitable jump for moguls, where you need a very accurate spot to land. Great speed is required off smaller ramps, though.

Methodical Introduction to the Misty Flip

Now we will learn a basic 540° Misty Flip progression that is simple and can be used to progress into other off-axis tricks. This progression can be made safer by placing a mat on the back half of the trampoline or by having a coach toss a throw pad. Only after you feel comfortable performing seat drops, back drops, and airplane maneuvers, should you move on to this Misty Flip progression. It is recommended that this trick be performed under the supervision of a professional coach, who can help facilitate the process and help keep you safe.

Athlete: David Babic. Photographer: Dan Starke. Location: Park City. UT Misty 720°

To begin, warm up with a few forward rolls on a mat. Once you have this feeling, try another roll, but this time tuck your right shoulder in toward your left knee as you roll (this motion is for a person spinning to the left, reverse the movement for a right spin). The tuck will create a side rotation and will bring you onto your left hip as you return upright. At this point, continue to rotate your hips and shoulders to the left so that you finish facing in the opposite direction from where you started. This is the basic movement of the Misty Flip and D Spin, which we will discuss later. It is essential that you have a good grasp of this role before moving onto the trampoline.

Now that you have the roll down, try it with a bit of air under you. The takeoff begins with an even lift-off on both feet, photo 1. Once in the air, initiate the forward roll by dropping the right shoulder forward, toward your left knee (reverse this motion if you want to spin to the right), photo 2. This motion will bring your feet up into the air and drop your head toward the trampoline. Spot the trampoline and rotate onto your back, photo 3. Some athletes try to land on the small of their back with their head up and feet rotated 270° from their starting position, photo 4. Lifting back off the trampoline, your whole body should continue to rotate, spinning to the left, photo 5. As you finish your rotation, your head should come back up with your feet finding a balanced position beneath you.

Athlete: David Babic. Photographer: Dan Starke. Location: Park City. UT Misty 540° Drill

Once you have a firm grasp of this move, you can negate the bounce on your back and perform the entire move in one single bounce. I would recommend using a throw pad, foam pit, swimming pool or landing on a pad for your first attempts at the entire move. With practice, you will be on your way to developing a repertoire of New School tricks.

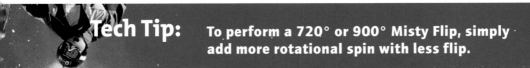

Tech Tip: To perform a 720° or 900° Misty Flip, simply add more rotational spin with less flip.

Misty Flip with Skis

Photo 1 of the on water sequence shows that even during the takeoff, a slight forward rotation is possible. Don't forget that the takeoff should still be from two feet in an up and outward direction. It is up to you to decide which direction you prefer to turn. Those who turn to the left in the heli, will look over their left shoulder.

As you dive out with a slight front flip rotation, begin to drop your right shoulder towards your left knee (for a left spinning rotation). As you rise off the jump continue to drop your shoulder towards your knee (photo 2). Once you roll onto your back you will be able to see the sky and your feet and head will be evenly forward (photo 3).

Now that you have reached the apex of your jump, your body will continue to spin and your feet will begin to lead the rest of your body towards the landing (photo 4). Once you reach 540° of rotation you will begin to spot the ground and prepare for landing (photo 5).

As in a normal front flip, it is important to pull through with your heels. As you do this, make sure that you keep looking over your left shoulder to follow the rotation to square landing (photo 6).

8.2   D Spin 720°

The D-Spin is an off-axis jump that goes past the horizontal plane but does not reach a completely inverted state.

Methodical Introduction to the D Spin
Once you have learned the 540° Misty Flip progression on the trampoline (see Misty 8.1), you will have the basics needed to perform the infamous D Spin! As with the Misty

Athlete: David Babic. Photographer: Dan Starke. Location: Park City. UT D-Spin 720°

Flip, this progression can be made safer by placing a mat on the back half of the trampoline or having a coach toss a throw pad. Only after you feel comfortable performing seat drops, back drops and airplane maneuvers, should you move on to this D Spin progression. I recommend performing this progression under the supervision of a professional coach who can help facilitate this process and keep you safe.

Essentially, a D Spin is a 540° Misty Flip that has a 180° spin added to the beginning of the trick. To begin, warm up with a few forward and backward rolls on a mat. Once you have this feeling, do a few Misty Flip simulation rolls by tucking the shoulder (See Misty Flip 8.1). Now, do the D Spin roll by first standing prepared to do a backward roll. As you lower into the roll, slowly rotate your hips and shoulder 180° to the left (reverse this move if you want to spin to the right). Once you are facing backwards, tuck your right shoulder in toward your left knee as you roll (this motion is where the misty flip begins). The tuck will create a side rotation and bring you onto your left hip as you return upright. At this point, continue to rotate your hips and shoulders to the left so that you finish facing in the same direction from where you started. It is essential that you have a good grasp of this sequence before moving onto the trampoline.

Now that you have the roll down, try it with a bit of air under yourself. The takeoff begins with an even lift-off on both feet. Initiate the rotation with your shoulders, twisting them to the left (reverse this motion if you want to spin to the right) and set a little bit of flip using your center of mass (COM), photo 1. Once in the air and 180° has been achieved, initiate the forward roll by dropping the right shoulder forward, toward your left knee, photo 2.

This motion will bring your feet up into the air and drop your head toward the trampoline. Spot the trampoline and rotate onto your back. Try to land on the small of your back with your head up and feet rotated 90° from their starting position, photo 3. Lifting back off the trampoline, your whole body should continue to rotate, spinning to the left, photo 4. When your feet come back underneath your body, use this time to adjust for your landing, photo 5. As you finish your rotation, your head should come back up, with your feet finding a balanced position beneath you, photo 6.

Once you have a firm grasp of this move, you can eventually negate the bounce on your back and perform the entire move in one single bounce. I would recommend using a throw pad, foam pit, swimming pool or landing on a pad for your first attempts at the entire move.

Athlete: David Babic. Photographer: Dan Starke. Location: Park City. UT D-Spin 7 Dril

Skier: David Babic
Photo: Patrick Reeves

D Spin with Skis

Phase 1. Entrance

See T Set Phase 1.

Phase 2. Takeoff

It is recommended that the straight 720° maneuver be learned and developed before attempting this trick. With a strong stance, the athlete begins to resist the pressure on the jump, straightening the body at the end of the jump. At this point, the movements of the upper and lower body separate slightly. The lower body finishes the takeoff in the same manner as the T-set. With the skis tracking straight off the jump, the hips line up over the knees and the balls of the feet. The lower body should be perpendicular to the curve of the jump (This is the main difference between upright and off-axis jumps with backwards rotation). To create a D-spin, often you will need to initiate a slight back flip set on the takeoff. The body moving with the jump angle will generate some flip rotation, creating the off-axis flight. At this point, the upper body should begin a slight rotation in the direction that it wants to spin, led by even shoulders and head. With more flip initiation, the trick will have less rotation than a straight 720°. On takeoff, the eyes may be looking down or behind the athlete, but as the athlete spins into the air he may lose sight of the ground and see the sky. If the trick is done with a large amount of flip, the ground can be seen almost throughout.

Tech Tip:

Off-axis flight

To create more off-axis angle: initiate more flip movement into the takeoff. Leaning back more on the jump will create more flip and thus more off-axis.

To create less off-axis angle: stand more forward on takeoff. Often, simply lifting your vision during the takeoff will help this action. If you are looking at the ground during takeoff, try spotting a bit higher, (maybe spotting behind you on takeoff will stand you more upright) thus lessening your off-axis angle. This is how the Cork 720° is performed. Use the same takeoff with higher vision and less flip.

Phase 3. Trick

As the athlete lifts off the jump, his skis should continue to track straight but begin to rotate from the shoulders' initiation. The shoulders should continue to rotate as they drop down, slightly behind the body. The head and vision drop with shoulders, spotting behind or below the athlete, depending on amount of flip desired. With the head square between the shoulders, the eyes should be looking straight in front of the body, helping to keep your body in alignment while in the air. Once the upper body has moved through the first quarter of the rotation it is time for the lower body to catch up. Simply squeezing the stomach muscles allows the lower body to catch up, so that the all body parts are together moving as one. Pulling the lower body closer to your chest will give you greater control of the maneuver. The athlete can adjust the rotation speed by making his body longer or shorter. Outstretched arms will help to slow the spin, while pulling in the arms close to the body will speed up this movement. As the body moves through the first 360° spin, it will lose sight of the ground but it will come back into sight at 540°. During this maneuver, the head will start behind the feet as they move down the hill. While the body is spinning in the air, the feet and head will hopefully swap places (this is an important concept to understand for landing). Throughout the jump, the head will continue to lower while the feet rise. When the athlete reaches his apex, both the feet and head should be even. As the athlete descends, his head should now be leading his feet as they move down the hill. With the feet behind the rest of the body, the athlete will now have greater control for landing.

Phase 4. Landing

When the athlete has reached 540° of rotation (1 and 1/2 full spins), the athlete can begin to prepare for the landing. Opening up at 540° helps the athlete slow the rotation of the jump and prepare for landing. The athlete can be looking down slightly, to spot his landing as he approaches the ground. Depending on your jump speed and amplitude, you can adjust your foot position to maximize your landing potential. With this trick, you will have some flip and spin momentum that must be dealt with on landing. To adjust for this additional momentum, land with your feet slightly behind where you would for a straight jump. Upon landing, quickly pick your eyes up and look down the fall line to see what is ahead.

8.3 Back Full

Learning Back Full on Trampoline

One of the best ways to learn this trick on a trampoline is with the aid of a mat or a spotting rig. To use a mat, simply place it on the back half of the trampoline and project yourself onto the mat for a soft landing. If you do not have access to these devices, try using a number of bed tricks, e.g., seat drops, back drops, or airplane maneuvers, and have sufficient confidence with performing a straight back flip with a layout position. Only after you have learned these tricks and feel comfortable performing them should you move on to this back full progression.

To begin, warm up with a few seat drops, back drops and airplane bed tricks to get your control and balance up. Now that you are comfortable, we will begin by attempting to execute a 180° spin with a 3/4 back flip. The trick starts similarly to a straight back flip, but with a bit less flip. Focus on lifting your center, with even pressure on each foot (see photo 1). Once you have a good clean lift, you can begin to drop the arm in the direction you wish to spin (drop left arm to spin left, right arm to spin right; see photo 2). An arm drop and a slight twist in the shoulder is all that is needed to initiate rotation. At this point, you can quickly spot the trampoline, to gauge your height and speed (photo 3). Keep a neutral head and use your arms to control your rotation, as you guide your body back to the trampoline (photo 4). Tuck your head just before landing and stay relaxed as you enter the tramp (photo 5). Try to land facing the opposite direction from which you started (photo 6). If your body is

Athlete: David Babic. Photographer: Dan Starke. Location: Park City. UT   Back 1/2 Dr

not in line with the trampoline, chances are you rushed your takeoff or had a one-footed takeoff. Caution: This is an advanced drill; only practice this movement under the supervision of a professional. It is recommended that a throw pad be used for the first attempts.

Jump Description Full

Athlete: David Babic. Photographer: Dan Starke. Location: Park City. UT Back Full

The Back Full is essentially a laid out back flip with a full 360° spin throughout.

On the Trampoline

As with the partial full (180° spin, with 3/4 back flip), it is important to warm up with a number of bed tricks. These warm-ups help to increase your overall control and balance, both of which are essential for this trick. Once you are comfortable, you will begin an attempt to execute a complete back full on a trampoline (a 360° spin with a full back flip). In order to complete the full trick, you will need to execute the complete back full with more height than was requried to perform the partial full. To gain the additional height, a few additional bounces may be required prior to the jump execution. As before, focus on lifting your center, with even pressure on each foot (see photo 1).

You will want to start your backward rotation in the same manner as if performing a straight back flip. Once you have a good clean lift, you can begin to drop the arm in the direction you wish to spin (drop left arm to spin left, right arm to spin right; see photo 2). An arm drop and a slight twist in the shoulders is all that is needed to initiate rotation. At this point, you can quickly spot the trampoline to gauge your height and speed (photo 3). You will want to make sure that you have enough rotational speed to complete the full 360° rotation.

As previously stated, you can slow your rotation speed by raising your arms out to the sides or increase the rotation by bringing your arms in closer. Maintain a neutral head as you guide your body back to the trampoline (photos 4 and 5). Try to land evenly on both feet, facing the same direction as you started (photo 6). If you did not have enough backwards rotation, you should increase your initial lift during takeoff.

Skier: David Babic
Photo: Patrick Reeves

ON Skis

Phase 1. Entrance

See Back Flip Set Phase 1.

Phase 2. Takeoff

This takeoff is similar to the straight back flip. It is recommended that the straight back flip in a laid position be mastered, with a good understanding of how to control the jump, before this trick is attempted. As the athlete reaches the end of the jump, his body should be moving in a perpendicular fashion with the curve of the jump. Flip rotation can be initiated from the shoulders and or feet, but the most consistent method is to lift the trick from your core, or Center of Mass (COM). Projecting your COM up into the air gives height and control to the flip. This lifting method prevents the tendency to sling the trick. A strong core will assist in bringing the feet with the rest of the body, so that all body parts are flipping together as one. A slight arm movement can assist the takeoff and will help to initiate the rotation. I would recommend keeping the arm swing similar to the T-set movement. It is important to keep your vision forward, looking past the jump and down the hill during takeoff. The head should be balanced over the shoulders and the rest of the body.

Common Mistakes:

1 Leading the flip with your head. Causes the rest of your body to be left behind, stall out, or sling by landings. To fix, try to keep your head forward longer and focus on flipping from your belly button. Also, if stalling is a problem, try driving your feet more on takeoff.
2 Slinging. Caused by the overambitious attempting to land fuzzy side up! Results in over rotation and a sore back and neck. To fix, focus on a lifting the trick higher into the air. Another remedy is to try to spot your skis throughout the first half of the trick.

3 Sucking up the takeoff. A fear of amplitude and commitment can result in Low Unidentified Flying Objects (LUFOs), which in turn result in many short crashed landings. This result is caused by a soft takeoff, usually in the hips and knees, at the takeoff point of the jump. To fix: simply stand stronger against the jump and allow yourself to carry higher into the air.

Phase 3. Trick

As the athlete lifts off the jump, his skis should continue to track straight but begin to rotate as the shoulders and vision initiate rotation. The shoulders should continue to rotate as they drop in down, directly behind the body. The head and vision drop with shoulders, spotting below the athlete. With the head square between the shoulders, the vision should be looking straight in front of the body, which helps to keep your body in alignment while in the air. As the upper body moves through the first quarter of the rotation, the body should be moving as one, in a straight, pinned out position.

As the body flips and rotates, the athlete should be able to comfortably spot the ground in front of him and make adjustments to deal with the flip's speed and amplitude. The athlete can adjust his rotation speed by making his body bigger or smaller. Outstretched arms will help to slow the spin, while pulling in the arms close to the body will speed up the movement.

During this maneuver, the head will start behind the feet as he moves down the hill. While the body is spinning in the air, the feet and head will hopefully swap places (this is an important concept to understand for landing). Throughout the jump, the head will continue to lower while the feet rise. When the athlete reaches the apex, the feet should be directly over the head. As the athlete descends, his head should now be leading the feet as they move down the hill. With the feet behind the rest of the body, the athlete will now have greater control for landing.

Phase 4. Landing

When the athlete has reached the 180° position of their flip and spin (1/2 back flip and 1/2 full spin), the athlete can begin to prepare for the landing. The athlete should be looking down slightly, to spot his landing as he approaches the ground. Depending on your speed and amplitude, you can adjust your foot position to maximize your landing potential. With this trick, you will have a lot of flip and a little spin momentum that must be dealt with upon landing. To adjust for this momentum, land with your feet slightly behind where you would for a straight jump. Upon landing, quickly pick your vision up and look down the fall line to see what is ahead.

8.4 Rodeo 540°

Sven Küenle, German Freeski pro, will present the Rodeo 540° after we get to know him better in a short interview.

The life of the 20-year-old out of Stuttgart, Germany has revolved around grabs, flips and spins since he left high school. As a newcomer, he is right at the top of the international scene as far as style and nonchalance are concerned. Despite being busy with film and photo productions in America, he still found time to give us a few tips.

Hi Sven, how did a boy from Stuttgart get into this sport?

I actually got involved with the sport thanks to my father, who put me on skis when I was three years old, and from then on I didn't want to get off! As all my friends are snowboarders, in 2000 I just tried to do the jumps on skis that they were doing on their snowboards.

What have been your best experiences until now?

My best skiing experiences were the days in the Whistler back country with extremely fresh snow and being able to ski the whole day by myself in the same place.

Which is your favorite New School discipline ?

I don't want to limit myself to only one; I think that freeskiing just means that you can enjoy both the park and free riding.

Skier: Sven Küehle
Foto: poachers-mag.com.
Location: Zugspitze

In what way do you think the scene is different in America than in Europe?

In America, they are a couple of years ahead and therefore a great deal bigger. From the point of view of the resorts, there are better facilities in the USA. They build very good parks, better than most in Europe.

What motivates you? What are your goals?

My motivation is my love of sport. Skiing is my life and I will do anything to be able to continue skiing. My goals for the future are definitely to go on filming as much as I can. That is my main priority. The competitions are secondary for me.

Do you see yourself as a competitor or is the work of a Freeski pro more like being a stuntman for various film and photo productions?

As I already said, I am someone who falls into the category of stuntman for film and photo productions.

Have you ever had any nasty injuries? How do you protect yourself?

Just a short while ago, I hurt my knee. That was really bad, as overloading caused the injury. I can ski again now, but I am always very careful and tape my knee. Also, I go over very carefully in my mind what I am going to do before I jump or ski a line.

What advice can you give a young New Schooler who wants to have a career as a pro like you?

My tip is that you shouldn't overestimate yourself and you should ski thoughtfully, because a professional skier's main asset is his body. So, go for it, but don't overdo it, otherwise you may have to stop completely and be out for a whole season.

Jump Description for the Rodeo 540°

Before you can try the Rodeo 540°, you must have mastered kicker jumps and the basics, like 180° and 360°. It also helps if you can already land perfectly switch (backwards), which you can best practice with the 180° and 540°. As soon as you feel ready with kicker jumps, you are ready to jump a Rodeo 540°.

The most important thing is that you can picture the jump in your mind, i.e., that the whole movement sequence is clear to you, before you actually jump.

When you are ready, check your speed on the kicker a couple of times by jumping straight so that you make sure you land perfectly.

Then ski nice and relaxed onto the kicker. On takeoff, twist your body in the usual direction and make a sideways movement at the same time, as if you are letting your body fall to the side. Make sure, though, that you do actually takeoff. In the photos, you can see how I twist my right shoulder down to the right below my ski tip.

When you are in the air, grip your ski and hold the grab for as long as possible so that the trick looks smooth and stylish. At the start of the jump, you will not be able to see the landing area. Stay calm in the air, though, and prolong the rotation until you can see the landing area. As soon as you can see it, release the grab and get ready for a switch landing. Land and bring the trick home!

The Rodeo 540° is my absolute favorite trick because it is so smooth and stylish. This trick also gives you a gigantic feeling in the air, as the trajectory is so rounded.

Have fun, Sven

You must have the trick very clear in your head so that you just have to reel it off. Whatever you do, don't just ski onto the kicker and hope for the best! **TIP**

Athlete: David Babic. Photographer: Dan Starke. Location: Park City. UT

Skier: Sven Küenle
Foto: k2sports.de
Location: Zugspitze

⑨ SPECIAL SKIING TECHNIQUES

As we already know, skiers of all abilities can learn New School tricks. You don't necessarily need perfect ski technique for your first small jumps. Start with a secure approach, ski into the jump, and develop balance in the air and land on both feet, slowing down using the wedge.

Many people set their goals even higher and want to show several different tricks in one run, as in other sports like surfing or skating. They should try the halfpipe, slopestyle or the moguls with two ski jumps. For this style, you need special ski techniques, though.

With this in mind, we have been able to get two guest authors for our book that will introduce you to the Halfpipe and Grinding Rails. Sven Küenle, one of the few German New School pros, will take you through your first steps in the halfpipe and explain what you should watch out for there.

Ruben Wellinger, from Garmisch, Germany, gives valuable tips for grinding on all kinds of rails in the funparks. Finally, Gerhard will explain how to ski moguls in detail.

This is not the place to go into ski techniques like powder snow or off-piste skiing – also called big mountain – although New School jumps over rocks are also used in Freeskiing. This discussion would be beyond the scope of this book.

If you want to deal with these subjects, you need to look at a thorough description of the powder snow ski technique, jumping over rocks and landing in different conditions as well as the natural hazards of the high mountains.

This alone would probably fill a whole book. Perhaps in the future you can find an experienced Freeskier and mountain guide who can help you with this. There is already a great deal of literature on the mountains available, although it is not really geared toward young people.

Have fun and be successful with our training and technique tips
from Sven Küenle, Ruben Wellinger and Gerhard Blöchl

9.1 Riding the Halfpipe

You must be a good skier and already be able to do simple jumps from a kicker in order to learn to ride the halfpipe.

The first time you ride a halfpipe, you should set the first attempt up so that you enter the pipe from the bottom, i.e., you don't drop in right from the top of the halfpipe wall. Instead, work your way up each side of the wall and only ride up the big walls of ice as high as you feel comfortable. Repeat this a few times and each time try to go a little higher up each wall.

When you have a few runs behind you and feel secure, you can practice riding up to the top rim, called the coping. To do this, you have to start higher up the walls. Take care that you ride onto the rim with pressure so that you don't slip on the hard walls and always put your bodyweight on the bottom ski.

When you have enough momentum to be able to reach the coping, make a small hop at the rim and turn through almost 180° so that you ride forward into the halfpipe again and can do the same thing on the other side. To get a feeling for this, you should repeat it a few times.

Halfpipe riding has a lot to do with feeling, and it has to be developed for every pipe. Each pipe is different, so it can be very dangerous to go full on without knowing beforehand how the pipe is shaped.

The problem with the halfpipe is that the landing area is very restricted, as you always have to land where the halfpipe is steepest, i.e., directly below the coping. If the halfpipe is a little too flat at takeoff, the rider will not fly vertically upward, but make a trajectory that takes him above the coping, and he will land on the flat part on top, which can be very painful. If the halfpipe is too steep, it keeps you inside and you land inside the pipe.

If you have practiced your runs so that you feel more confident, you can familiarize yourself with the thought of jumping out of the halfpipe, making an air. For this, you should be absolutely sure that the halfpipe walls are vertical. When you start to build up more speed and ride higher up the walls, it is important to ride right up to the coping and to stand in a normal position on the skis.

Initially, you can use your poles to help you when you reach the copings, i.e., your left pole, when you ride up the right wall, and vice versa. DO NOT "push off" the copings though, otherwise you will fall into the center of the halfpipe. Do not "suck up" the takeoff either, or your will land on the deck above. In a well-shaped pipe, in principle, all you have to do is ride out and then land perfectly on the steep walls again.

As soon as you are in the air, make an arc with your pole and then land perfectly back on the steep wall of the pipe. Practice this action for as long as it takes, until you feel confident enough to attempt your first tricks.

If you are already so good that you can come more than 3ft. outside the halfpipe, you can try your first grab. It is up to you which part of the ski you grab. As soon as you feel sure enough, all the other tricks will happen by themselves. Just keep at it and train as much as possible!

In recent years, the development of the halfpipe has undergone a big change with the construction of so-called Superpipes. While about 10 years ago, a few snowboarders with shovels used to shape their own halfpipes, today there are special machines that are attached to the snow groomer and allow it to build big, perfectly shaped halfpipes.

This technological innovation meant that snowboarding became an Olympic discipline and that skiing in the halfpipe became spectacular, and led to breathtaking jumps and competitions such as the Halfpipe U.S. Open. The halfpipe is also part of the X-Games. Both of these events, the biggest on the international scene, attract an unbelievable media presence for halfpipe riding.

While many U.S. resorts already possess very good halfpipes, like Breckenridge, Colorado, in Europe the facilities are often lacking in the ski resorts. However, there are some good halfpipes, like in Zugspitze, or in some French resorts.

So, go for it and practice a lot, and we will see each other in the Halfpipe US Open!
– Sven Küenle

9.2 Grinding on Rails

Ruben Wellinger, Freeskier from Garmisch, Germany, will explain some interesting features of grinding below and give you some useful tips: The origins of grinding are in skateboarding. Skateboarders were the first to try to find a way of overcoming obstacles, like steps.

They tried just sliding across terrain and a new kind of skateboarding was born. The so-called rails were then constructed especially for this purpose, and they are now an established part of every skatepark. Snowboarders soon caught onto this idea and built their own rails in the snow.

Like the snowboarders who stole this idea from the skateboarders, skiers did the same to inline skaters, who made the rails in cities and parks their own with their various tricks way before New School skiing came along.

Skier: Ruben Wellinger
Photo: poachers-mag.com
Location: Zugspitze

Rails can be divided into two categories.

Urban rails are called handrails as they are intended to be barriers or for security and are not specifically built for grinding. These rails are usually very difficult to ride as they tend to be broken, damaged or completely unstable. There is often no space to get momentum either. But this is what makes handrails so exciting, as every rail produces new surprises and the rider is always pushed to his own limits.

Rails in terrain parks or skate parks are especially constructed for sliding. Many companies in the skate or snowboarding scene see this as a good chance to market their products by sponsoring a few rails in a park and putting their logo and/or slogan on them.

There are a large number of park rails of all different shapes and sizes. The basic shapes are the Straight Rail, which has no bends, as its name suggests, and the Kink Rail, which has a sharp downward bend after a few yards. These are very suitable for beginners, as it is very easy to learn grinding on them.

Most of the rails in the parks should only be ridden when you are better at sliding. These include the Rainbow Rail, an arc that is perpendicular to the ground that you can slide around; the C-Rail or Curved Rail, which is horizontal to the ground and upon which you slide a curve, and finally the S Rail, which is the C-Rail with an additional curve.

The most important things in grinding are keeping your balance and distributing your weight evenly over both feet, which can obviously be hard to do on an iron bar! That's why, for beginners, a wider surface like a wooden bench is more suitable, making grinding easier to learn. If a wooden bench is too easy for you, start with a wooden beam, as it is hurts less falling on wood than on iron or steel.

To slide on your chosen object, construct your ski jump beforehand so that you can easily slide off it and don't just plop down in an arc, because the edges of your skis will dig too deeply into the material. Always make sure, when grinding, that the edges of your skis are blunt and never smoothed/ground.

Your approach to the rail is also important. If it is too short, you will move too slowly, and it will be harder to keep your balance on the rail.

It is better to have too much momentum than too little, but with more experience and more rails conquered, you develop the feeling of how fast you need to go.

As in normal skiing, it is easier to keep your balance and to distribute your weight evenly over both feet if you bend your knees slightly and have a wide foot stance. So, do this in your approach and aim at the rail so that when you leave the ski jump, it is exactly between your legs. Takeoff from the jump and gain momentum in the 90° turn that you need in order to slide onto the rail at an angle.

According to the direction you turn in, you should land on the rail with either your left or your right foot forward. It is up to you in which direction you turn at takeoff, as everyone has his or her own favorite side. Your head remains in the same position during the takeoff, and your vision should be focused down along the rail out in front of you, as this helps you to place your skis centrally on the rail.

If you shift your weight too much onto your front foot, you will catch the edge in the rail and fall forward. If you shift your weight too much onto your back foot, you will tip over backward. The art of grinding consists of finding the happy medium.

Compared to the approach, takeoff and grinding, the landing is very easy. Once you get to the end of the rail, if you have done everything right, the landing takes care of itself.

There are obviously different kinds of takeoff and landing that an experienced rider can learn gradually. For example, you can approach backward instead of forward; make various turns, like a 270° instead of a 90° onto the rail. It is also possible to land backward or add another turn at the end of the rails. Putting your bad foot forward can also increase your trick repertoire, which is called unnatural. The possibilities open to the rider here are endless.

Have fun!
Ruben Wellinger

9.3 Skiing the Moguls

Wouldn't it be great if you could just sail down the dreaded moguls just as easily as you do on a groomed trail? There are mogul runs in nearly every ski resort. Especially in recent years, the number of natural mogul slopes has increased dramatically, which is due to more and more slopes being left as unprepared Freeride trails. The moguls are then formed naturally after a few days.

These trails present a real challenge for many skiers, for although skiers enjoy carving, it soon becomes boring on the prepared slopes. And who is lucky enough to get the whole slope to themselves, with the ability to push it right to the limit?

On the moguls, everyone can quickly test their own limits. For sure, there are always some skiers who shun this kind of bumpy trail, so that they don't, in their eyes, cut a bad figure when skiing off-piste or on moguls. But on the leveled slopes, they feel like the greatest and bravest amateur skiers. The point is that when you ski moguls, the difference in ability of a World Cup skier seems

much more drastic in real life than in downhill skiing. It doesn't matter if you can't quite ski on the edges down the slopes every time, you still secretly feel like Hermann Maier! The actual difference in ability between Joe Average-skier and world class downhill racers or freestyle pros, such as the ones normally seen on TV, is the same, though. On the moguls, it will be brought home to you after only a few yards.

The good recreational skier must first accept this fact, so that he is not constantly disappointed in his performance and can instead focus on making rapid progress. To make it easier for you to accept, we would like to show you the following image, which shows the difference in our perception more clearly.

If we consider the Men's and Women's Downhill World Cup, the layperson will not really appreciate the enormous difference in ability between the men and women. Actually though, there is a world of difference in terms of physiology and anatomy between a Janice Kostelic, and Hermann Maier or Darron Rahlves. In the Freestyle Moguls World Cup though, the same difference between men and women is much more obvious compared to the downhill event.

Skier: David Babic
Photo: Patrick Reeves

With this knowledge in the back of your mind, you must not get upset if you don't look like the best skier in the world out on the moguls. There are very few other sports where you can make such fast progress and experience real happiness when you can handle the moguls better and better every day. The technique for skiing moguls is a must for nearly all freeskiers and good skiers, as it is a good foundation for acquiring the ability to anticipate.

Anticipation here means the adaptation and preemption of a sporting movement and can be explained most easily in terms of tennis. A good player's anticipation allows him to know from the moment that his opponent hits the ball, which direction he should run. He can now preempt the action and run to the right place on the court from which he can return the ball perfectly. A player without such good anticipation often gets to the right place too late and returns many balls badly or doesn't even reach them at all.

It is this ability that separates the average skier from the good and great. In skiing, the terrain changes constantly. Good anticipation allows you to use the right technique, reacting correctly in good time and make every look safe and easy, however unfavorable and varying the conditions may be. This is equally true for racers, freeskiers, New Schoolers in the park and in the pipe, for telemarkers and also for the recreational skier.

This ability is sometimes wrongly called experience, but there is no reason that I have to ski for ten years before I can acquire this ability. This ability can be specifically learned in mogul schools and a lot of progress can be made in a short time. That is why it should be a reason for all skiers to dabble in on some of the many mogul runs.

It is not by accident that many top freeskiers, like the Canadian Shane McConkey for whom the smallest error on a descent studded with rocks could have fatal consequences, in the past, frequently entered mogul competitions in the context of a Mogul Pro Tour or the FIS.

Skiing moguls will serve to improve all of your skiing skills, for it is one of the most complex and spectacular ski disciplines.

Since the FIS rule change, the sport has been revolutionized now that all new-school overhead maneuvers have been allowed. Mogul skiing is now, quite simply, the Olympic New School discipline. Freestyle athletes, from over 26 nations, have been showing all kinds of New School maneuvers in the World Cup mogul events since the World Cup season of 2002-03, while they sprint down the bumps at a breathtaking speed.

The combination of old and new jumps provides an unbelievable diversity for the spectator. The days when the skiers could be judged on how well they performed their triple or quadruple twister are long gone. The New School movement has meant that the basic philosophy of freestyle is back, so that moguls now involve the most creative and varied tricks combined with athleticism. The modern trend is for many athletes to deliberately create their own jumps to attract the judges' attention. The judges evaluate the runs both in individual and parallel contests (elimination races, one-on-one in a knock out system) with points. The athletes receive points in three categories: 50% for ski technique on the moguls, 25% for air from both jumps, and 25% for the time.

For all those who have acquired a taste for moguls, Gerhard will now make a concise presentation of the mogul skiing technique.

Skier: Gerhard Blöchl
Photo: Armin Blöchl

We should first of all mention that there are different kinds of mogul runs. They can be roughly divided into three groups: natural moguls, prepared moguls and machine moguls. Natural moguls occur automatically on unrolled slopes. Both the distance between the moguls and their height are arbitrary and irregular. Specially prepared moguls, on the other hand, are pretty regular. Finally, machine moguls can be found mainly in World and North American Cup races. These are prepared mechanically with snow cats to provide big, regular bumps.

I have found that the ideal conditions in which to learn to ski moguls quickly are in Japanese ski resorts, where there are countless prepared mogul runs on very flat terrain. To start, it is better to avoid slopes that are too steep. You have to master the parallel short turn, and steep conditions can make this a difficult prospect. The turns should be about 10-15 ft. apart. Everyone should do their best to turn in the same place.

This is easiest to do by skiing in a small group, one after the other. If there are any problems with rhythm, cones or flags can be placed where each turn is to be made. With every run, the track becomes deeper and you will automatically improve. Now here is a basic technical model.

Basic Technique

The beginner should make sure that his body position is central. As with carving, your skis should be close together. The poles must be held in front of your body, as it is the position of the poles that usually determines success or failure for beginners. Don't forget: shorter poles are used for moguls.

Independently of the skier's level, a bending and stretching movement characterizes the skiing technique. It is the bending and stretching of your hips and knees, plus lateral sliding of your skis into each mogul, that allows you to control your speed.

Initially, it is more than enough if you only concentrate on these tips for body position and ski technique. Giving too much information at the start is counterproductive. Ideally, the moguls should be divided into short sections, and then skied with concentration and control. Only later can these sections be skied as a whole run.

Additional tips for natural moguls:
The first time you attempt a steep natural mogul slope, the highest priority is speed control. This basically happens between the bumps. By turning your skis across the fall

line, you will be able to control your speed. As you feel more comfortable, allow your skis to work more directly down the fall line. The basic technique is still just the same, though.

Progressive Technique

All those who are now able to master the most diverse moguls with the basic technique, can now set about learning the details of the fine form. You can improve your body position by always keeping your head up and looking down the fall line so that you can see the next 4 -6 moguls, depending on your speed. Your arms are still held in front of your body and now make very short jabs with the poles that just help to keep the rhythm. Your upper body is upright and projects down the hill to allow maximum range of movement for your legs. The legs form a block, and the skis are parallel.

The idea is to move with the mogul, absorbing the bump contours by actively bending and stretching, allowing the skier constant contact with the snow. This is the only way to move fluidly without stress. This active legwork enables World Cup skiers to control their speed effectively by speeding up or slowing down as necessary.

The skier has two possible movement directions on the moguls. On the one hand, the legs move vertically up and down in a wave pattern, and on the other they move horizontally in an extremely narrow slalom from left to right. The art of good skiing is to carry out both movements simultaneously, while keeping the upper body almost static.

At the deepest point of the mogul trough, your legs are almost completely straight (photo 2 of the sequence). You negotiate the next mogul by actively pulling your heels up under your backside (photo 3). As you move past the moguls, you relax as the skis are turned into the new curve direction, and move from the crest of the mogul into the next trough.

This movement process from the crest of the mogul happens successfully when your hips carry over the bump with your feet tucked underneath. Now you are in a position to extend down the back of the mogul. Shifting your weight onto the front of your feet and pushing your shins against the tongue of your ski boots achieves this pressure. You then travel on the edge of the ski until the hips and knees are straightened into the deepest point of the trough (photo 4).

This technique becomes automatic during the course of the year and allows very high speed on the moguls without damaging your body.

Jumping on the Moguls

Like the jumps in the park, when you jump on the moguls, you should be aware that mogul jumps are usually shorter and have a stronger kick. This requires a significantly faster, more explosive takeoff. This also causes a steeper trajectory. However, the main difference is that there is no landing slope; you are jumping into more moguls. These landing conditions require a lot of confidence when you jump and an accurate landing spot.

Skier: Gerhard Blöchl
Photo: Armin Blöchl
Location: Zermatt

10 RISK MANAGEMENT

Skier: Armin Blöchl
Photo: Martin Trautmann
Location: Osterfelder

The New School sport is certainly a great deal more hazardous than say water aerobics. But as in many other adventure sports, that is exactly what makes the sport exciting.

Of course, we hope that our book has taught you to build up every overhead jump systematically and never to use a trial-and-error approach.

For flips with spins, we recommend that you find an experienced coach with either a gymnastics, trampolining or water jump background to help you, who can provide you with the right information in a few hours. It doesn't matter which method you choose or which coach you work with, there will always be a certain amount of risk involved.

That is exactly why we want to make you aware of the risks, for sayings like "Pain is temporary and glory is forever!" are completely inappropriate in a New School and freestyle context.

No jump, no matter how audacious, is worth broken bones, skull or vertebral injuries! Anyone who thinks that he is sufficiently protected just because he is wearing the compulsory protective gear, like a helmet and back protector, is very much mistaken.

Ultimately, you are responsible for your own safety! So before every ride or jump, you should go through the following points:

1. Have I checked the ski jumps using straight jumps, so that I can get enough height to do my planned trick and reach the landing area?

By checking, I establish my planned approach and mark the starting point. In case the temperature of the snow rises and the snow melts, I should check it again. The same is true if the temperature drops during the day.

2. Have I chopped and prepared the landing surface properly and is it free of objects (shovel, wooden posts, backpacks, skis...)? I must double check that the landing is safe. For off-piste airs in the powder snow, I have to check the landing area with avalanche probes, in case I am not familiar with the terrain from the summer. The most dangerous situation is when there is snow everywhere and you think you can jump without risk over all rocks and snow drifts. The rocks you are jumping over can hide smaller, sharper rocks that are covered by a layer of new snow.

3. Do I have the right movement experience for the trick I want to do and are the snow conditions right? Am I 100% sure?

The jumper must weigh all these factors individually before every jump. Of course, a mogul skier in the World Cup cannot prepare the landing area exactly as he would like and his run-out consists of a 2.5-4 ft. high, often icy mogul minefield. But he can calculate his risk, as he has already done it safely more than 100 times before.

However, someone who is doing the jump for the first time in the snow must make extra preparations. He needs a ramp with a steep and particularly soft sloping landing with a completely clear run-out. Individual risk management enables both athletes to achieve a similar, residual risk despite their difference in ability.

When looking at particularly spectacular New School jumps in films or magazines, you mustn't forget that these jumpers have an extremely high level of ability. They plan jumps over crevasses, roads or several snow cats with the utmost care – like a stuntman. Without good risk management, many of these stunts would end in tears.

Particularly Important:

There's always a point of no return!

After your personal risk assessment and as soon as you have definitely decided to jump, concentrate briefly as you run through the jump in your mind. Once you commit to the jump, proceed as planned!
If you brake during the approach or try to abort the jump, you risk not gaining the height and distance you need to do the trick. In the worst case, you could fall your back or even crash on the jump. These lead to the most dangerous crashes. It is better to over-rotate on a back flip than to under rotate and fall on your head!

Despite perfect risk management, you will not be able to avoid the odd light fall, as they are an unavoidable part of the learning process and must be accepted as part of the sport. We have already discussed this in Chapter 2.6 "Mental Preparation."

You Can Also Learn How to Fall

So that you don't get hurt, you must react correctly at the crucial moment. You should never just switch off and let destiny take over! Even when you fall, you must still retain body tension and a certain amount of overview.

If you over-rotate or land on the tails of your skis, to protect your joints, you shouldn't force the landing, but let yourself fall backward. The worst-case scenario is to land on your stomach and it must be avoided at all costs, as it can lead to an overextension of the vertebrae! If necessary, it is better to turn so you fall onto your side.

Don't worry! As you step up from small ramps to bigger ones, you will gradually get more experience and learn how to fall safely.

We hope we haven't frightened anyone, for bad accidents are usually rare. However, we want to be honest and prepare and advise you as well as possible. In that vein, Dr. Uwe Glatzmaier gives his contribution from an orthopedic point of view on the following pages.

In the next chapter, you can find out more about just how dangerous this sport is, or isn't. Then there are some important instructions for first aid in case of skiing accidents.

10.1 New School Skiing from a Medical Point of View

Dr. Uwe Glatzmaier is the team doctor for the German National Ski Freestyle Team, orthopedic surgian and consultant of the orthopedic department in the hostpital of the Barmherzigen Brüder, Munich, Germany.

New School and Mogul Skiing – Presentation of a New Sport and Its Health Aspects

Modern Skiing

In the past few years, skiing has developed in two directions.

The carving technique made possible by increasingly shaped skis has completely changed groomed trail skiing. High carve speeds combined with extreme radius allow good skiers to feel sensations that normally only powder snow skiers experience and also enable weaker skiers to carve on their edges.

However, on a critical note, there is an increased accident risk due to the diagonal motion at high speed, as well as accidents due to the skis twisting.

The other direction – also partly determined by the development of the ski industry – is known as New School skiing. This includes such disciplines as freeskiing (freeriding), slopestyle and also ski cross. The basis of these forms of terrain-adapted skiing is formed by mogul skiing, which has developed from being a form of "trick skiing" or "hotdog skiing" to an attractive, high performance competition sport.

Skier: Gerhard Blöchl
Photo: Armin Blöchl
Location: Kitzsteinhorn

Moguls for Everyone
New programs should encourage the attraction of moguls.

For example, in Switzerland the former Olympian Jörg Biner has developed a program called "Simply Moguls – Innovation with Tradition," in which limited grooming of the slopes in flat to moderate terrain creates simple, natural moguls. They promise that the benefits of this are principally that even inexperienced skiers can ski at low speeds, have less danger of collision than they would on a crowded slope and, last but not least, maintain good health due to the harmonious bending and stretching movement as the joints are weighted and unweighted.

Medical and Orthopedic Aspects
The often negative reports of the damage moguls do to your knees and back are unfounded from a medical and orthopedic point of view.

Previous studies, like the *Study of Selected Biomechanical Parameters of Moguls Skiing* by Anke Clauss (former German national squad athlete), show significantly less loading on the knee joint than previously thought. Electromyographic measurements monitoring muscular activity and coordination give maximal values for the final absorption phase with a quick fall in the extension phase. These values are clearly inferior to the measured compressive forces during the more static loading of carving at high speeds and small curve radius.

The Modern Mogul Technique, as used at competition level, is characterized by movement in the fall line with chopped swing turns at the sides of the moguls and a compact posture with an upright and and still upper body. The arms are held to the front of the body, the poles are held with loose wrists and there is maximal absorption of the mogul by actively bending and stretching the legs. The skis are close together and parallel and have as much contact with the snow as possible. This upright posture of the upper body in this technique requires a great deal of tension in the trunk muscles.

This, along with a maximal absorption on the mogul, clearly reduces the compression forces on the spine, particularly on the vertebrae and the small vertebral joints in the lower lumbar spine. Spreading the load evenly over both legs, plus the active bending and stretching leads to a rhythmic weighting and unweighting of the knee joint, especially of the cartilages and the ligaments. This causes a physiologically alternating load without the danger of increasing wear and tear. The risk of injury is also far lower than is commonly thought. At the grass roots level, you can often avoid crowded slopes, thus making collisions less likely. At low speeds, there are far fewer bad injuries. At competition level too, mogul skiing fares better than alpine skiing in direct comparison.

Skier: Gerhard Blöchl
Photo: Armin Blöchl
Location: Zermatt

Unlike alpine skiing, life-threatening or fatal injuries are unknown in moguls.

Scientific studies from the Oslo Sports Trauma Research Center from the Norwegian Team's Dr. Stig Heir in a long term observation over ten years and during the last two World Cup seasons show a slight increase in the number of cruciate ligament injuries in Mogul skiers. However, compared to alpine skiers, injuries are still less frequent.

On the team that I have been taking care of for five years, out of a squad of 14 athletes there have been nine serious injuries that necessitated a break from competition. This includes knee, collarbone and shoulder injuries. With each athlete having an average of 160 ski days per year, this corresponds to a frequency of 1.1 injuries per 1,000 ski days.

From this evaluation, it shows that mogul skiing, like alpine skiing, is still quite a dangerous sport, but it is still less dangerous than other skiing disciplines.

Above all, I want to counteract any prejudice that that may prevent youngsters from taking up this fascinating sport due to fear of injury.

10.2 First Aid – What to Do in Case of a Skiing Accident

Safeguarding the Scene of the Accident
About 10-20 yards above the injured person, stick 1 or 2 pairs of crossed skis in the snow. This should be done even on apparently clear or crowded slopes.

First Aid for the Injured Person
If the skis are still attached, take them off and place the injured person in the least painful position according to their condition (Be careful in the case of back injuries!). Do not remove the ski boots though. Then carry out the emergency measures according to the following guidelines.

Evacuation
If the injured person cannot make it down to the hill under his or her own volition, you will need the resort ski patrol. Alert the resort ski patrol with accurate information, especially about the scene of the accident and possible injuries.

First Aid Procedure

Understanding the Accident Situation
- **Environment:** Are there other injury hazards (other skiers, after effects of an avalanche, difficult terrain, crevasses, etc.)?

Is emergency rescue required (from a slope, a crevasse or an avalanche, etc.)?

- **The Injured:** Is he in a life-threatening condition (shock, breathing or heartbeat stopped)?

Emergency Measures

- **Checking Vital Functions:** consciousness – breathing – pulse

  a) By talking, touching and, if necessary, provoking a reaction by pinching.

  b) Checking breathing: stomach, hearing, sight, or feeling.

  c) Checking the pulse (wrist, neck):
     This can be difficult for many people, so look for other signs of life, such as spontaneous movements or swallowing.

- On suspicion of stopped breathing or heartbeat:
  - Start resuscitation measures (cardiopulmonary reanimation) see below.

- If the athlete is conscious:
  - Ask where he feels pain.
  - Can he move all his limbs (legs, arms)?
  - Can he breathe ok?

- **Bodycheck:**
  - Short, exploratory physical examination
  - Examine the head for wounds, bumps and bruises
  - Check the cervical spine carefully
  - Shoulders, thorax
  - Check the abdomen
  - Check the pelvic area
  - Move the legs about.

- If you have the slightest suspicion of **spinal injury**, if possible, the injured should not move at all, either passively or actively.
  - He should be evacuated ideally in a back board by professionals.
  - The cervical spine should be stabilized with a neck collar.
  - Transport, if possible, by trained ski rescue service, e.g., by using a folding stretcher.

– According to MD F. Brettner (own information)

The most important emergency measures in case of accidents that every helper should be familiar with are:

- **The correct body position**
- **Recognizing and eliminating possible life-threatening conditions**

More details on these two points are given below.

Correct Body Position of the Injured Skier

If you suspect a spinal injury, you should leave the injured in the position you found him in. He should also be transported in this position (ideally by back board). Unavoidable movements should be made extremely carefully without bending or twisting the spine (the danger of paralysis is low if you move very cautiously).

If you suspect a development of a state of shock, the injured should **immediately be put into the shock position**, i.e., raise the legs to increase the blood supply to the central and vital body organs.

Shock can develop easily, even in the case of a seemingly harmless accident (not only in the case of serious injury).

- Situations with a high risk of shock:
  - Bad weather
  - Fear
  - Cold
  - Exhaustion
  - Strong pain

- Particularly dangerous injuries:
  - Extreme blood loss
  - Internal injuries (skull, chest, stomach)
  - Deep broken bones

- Main Symptoms of Shock:
  - Pale complexion
  - Cold sweat
  - Racing, often undetectable, pulse

■ **Preventive measures**
As shock can be a very dangerous and insidious situation in the context of a skiing accident, you must think about preventing the development of shock in every accident by administering:

- Protection and warmth
- The most comfortable position possible
- Pain relief
- Constant observation and gentle evacuation

Life-Threatening Conditions (Lack of Breathing or Heartbeat)

Lack of breathing and heartbeat are usually found together. When breathing and heartbeat stop, for whatever reason, resuscitation must be started immediately.

■ **Free the airways.**

■ **Bend the head back slightly and elevate the chin.**

■ Block the lower jaw (press the thumbs from the outside in the angle between the upper and lower jaw).

■ Remove any foreign bodies (snow, mucus, vomit, blood, etc) with your bare hands. When the head is bent back, it allows the tongue to clear from the throat.

■ **1-2 quick breaths of mouth-to-mouth or mouth-to-nose respiration.**

■ Start cardiac massage.

■ Kneel down beside the thorax and cross both hands and place them on the sternum. Straighten your arms and then push down quickly and strongly 5-8 times.

■ Cardiac massage must be so effective that a weak pulse must be felt in the wrist.

■ **Rhythm of Combined Resuscitation:**
One helper method: 2 breaths   15 cardiac massages
Two helper method: 1 breath   5 cardiac massages

General Loss of Consciousness

As long as it is not accompanied by shock, lack of breathing or heartbeat, a loss of consciousness is not a life-threatening condition.

There can be problems for the helper if the cause of the loss of consciousness is not visible, e.g., skull injury, shock, heart attack, epilepsy.

Injury Theory

Bandaging
The principles for bandaging fresh wounds are:

- Don't touch the wound with your fingers. If possible, wear protective gloves.

- Don't wash with water.

- Don't use powders or ointments.

- Never remove foreign bodies or move protruding parts of the body (bones, soft tissue).

- Lay the patient down or at least make him lean against something while sitting down.

- A physician should see every serious wound within six hours!

In the case of heavy bleeding or even spurting wounds, create a tourniquet by placing a gauze bandage as a pad over the wound and fixing it with a firm bandage under pressure.

Steadying
Temporary braces with objects found at the scene of the accident should only be used if there is no organized transport for the patient (mountain rescue, slope rescue, etc.), i.e., only in exceptional cases.

Every improvised stretcher always carries a risk of injury!

Special Injuries
- **Skin Injuries**
  (See "Bandaging")

- **Blunt Injuries**
  Blunt injuries are caused by the application of external forces, where the skin is undamaged but the underlying structures (muscles, bones, ligaments, internal organs, etc.) are more or less seriously damaged.

- **Bruising, Sprains, Strains, etc.**
  Characteristics: Swelling, pain and restricted movement.
  First aid: horizontal position, possible rest.

- **Dislocations**
  A dislocation (usually of the shoulder) usually damages the joint capsule or the ligament. In the shoulder, the top of the arm bone comes out of its socket, usually forward and down, and remains in this abnormal position. Dislocations can sometimes be combined with broken bones.

  Characteristics
  - Change in the shape of the joint (touch the joint).
  - Joint movements are usually restricted or extremely painful.
  - At worst, sensation problems in the hand area due to pressure of the dislocated arm bone on the arm nerves.

  First Aid
  - A dislocated shoulder should not be put back by a lay person in an emergency, even if medical help will not be available for several hours, because an incorrect setting technique or the presence of undiagnosed associated broken bones can cause serious nerve and vascular damage.

- **Broken Bones**
  Symptoms
  - Abnormal mobility
  - Shape deviation
  - Pain under pressure
  - Open wound
  - Bone friction

In the case of open broken bones, the wounds are bandaged, and then the treatment is as for closed broken bones. The limb is placed in the least painful position and splinted if necessary. Do not reset it; just perform rough axial correction by careful pulling.

Special Types of Fracture

■ **Broken Rib**

Caused by a powerful force on the chest. They are usually very painful, especially during breathing and all other upper body movements.

■ **Fractured Spine**

As it is not possible to ascertain at the scene of the accident whether a painful spine is broken or just bruised, any first aid care must be done extremely gently.

Characteristics

- Pain in the area of the spine.
- Possible paralysis and/or sensation disturbance.

If you have any reason to suspect an injury to the spine, it is best to leave the patient in the position in which he was found if possible!

Absolutely necessary movements should be made extremely gently, without bending or twisting the spine. A person with an injured spine should be moved "in block", i.e., the body moved as a whole.

Several people place their hands underneath the injured person and lift him on a command onto a prepared backboard or slide the board underneath him. During the lifting, in the area of the presumed fracture, there should always be a **hollow back**.

If possible, the injured should be evacuated by helicopter.

In the case of an injury to the **cervical spine**, a rolled up blanket or item of clothing should be placed behind the neck so that the head is overextended and stabilized while leaning backward.

Internal Injuries

■ **Skull Injuries**

The seriousness of a skull injury is determined by the associated injury to the brain, and not to the skull itself.

Concussion *(Commotio cerebri)*

Characteristics: Temporary loss of consciousness, vomiting, lapse of memory, possible headache.

Cranio-cerebral bruising *(contusio cerebri)*

Characteristics: As for concussion, however loss of consciousness for more than one hour and possible difference in pupil size.

Basal Skull Fracture

Characteristics: Bleeding from the mouth and nose or ears, bruising around the eyes. Not necessarily loss of consciousness.

First Aid for all mentioned skull injuries

- Keep the head up (stable side position in the case of loss of consciousness)
- Constantly watch out for symptoms of life-threatening states (lack of breathing or heartbeat).

■ **Chest Injuries**

When a person has trouble breathing after a blow or fall onto the chest, or spits up bright red foamy blood, there could be a possibility of a lung injury, perhaps caused by fractured ribs penetrating the lungs.

This enables air to enter the chest and lungs, and a lung can even collapse. This is a dangerous impediment to breathing.

Lay on the injured side, so that the pressure is taken off the healthy side thus making breathing easier.

Open chest injuries with the sound of air can be closed with an airtight band-aid.

■ **Abdominal Injuries**

Injuries to the internal abdominal organs (e.g., ruptured spleen) are often overlooked, but they can be life threatening due to internal bleeding.

Characteristics:
- Hard, painful abdomen (the person squirms with pain), nausea and/or vomiting.
- Shock symptoms with increasing loss of blood.

First Aid:
Give nothing to eat or drink, relax the abdomen by bending the legs. If necessary, place the victim in the shock position.

In the case of an open abdominal injury, do not remove any foreign bodies or "stick in" protruding stomach contents. Just securely bandage the abdominal wound as you found it.

11 MOGULS – FREESTYLE GOES NEW SCHOOL

Under pressure from many athletes, most notably the 1998 Olympic Champion Jonny Moseley, the FIS moved with the times and changed the rules for the Olympic Moguls event. Ski Cross and the New School halfpipe disciplines were added to the Freestyle World Cup program. For the time being, the Olympic program only includes the freestyle disciplines of moguls and aerials.

As the international New School scene includes many former mogul skiers, it is not surprising that New School jumps are now shown in the Olympic Moguls discipline. It was a logical step by the FIS to recognize this progressive development in ski sports and to allow the new off-axis jumps in the Olympic Freestyle Discipline.

Freestylers had previously always been attracted by new developments, as they often felt constricted by the strict regulations of the competition jumps with increasing numbers of athletes.

Skier: Gerhard Blöchl
Photo: Karin Arnold
Location: World Cup Naeba (JPN)

Inspired by their snowboarder friends, many tried to do the same tricks in the halfpipe or to do jumps from kickers in the terrain parks, and the New School movement was born. At the forefront of this movement was the Canadian national freestyle team, including J.P. Auclair, J.F. Cusson and Vincent Dorion, who helped the ski manufacturer Salomon market the first twintips.

However, the New School movement has had little influence on the freestyle aerials discipline. They do have similar origins, but aerials have more in common with gymnastics and trampolining, where the aim is to reach an unbelievably high standard of perfection. Here, the priority is not individuality and stylish jumping, but rather the highest possible perfection and body tension, as in springboard diving.

Photo: Gerhard Blöchl
Location: World Cup Ruka (FIN)

The World Cup aerial events today feature triple flips with four spins or even more. The ski-jump facilities are standardized and they catapult the jumper to heights up to 50-60 feet. Despite great enthusiasm from spectators, like in competitive gymnastics, it has been difficult to encourage participation at the grass roots level, as the event is already very near the limit of human possibility.

There are also more and more up-and-coming jumpers from the high-performance centers of the sport, who interrupt their years of sporting development in order to emerge as shooting stars in the new school scene in Big Air competitions.

We greatly admire these aerialists, as well as training and competing along side them at training facilities or World Cup competition.

The next FIS Freestyle Winter Olympic Games take place in 2006 in Torino, Italy. The Moguls and Aerials events will be held at these Olympic games. Alongside these events, the halfpipe and skicross will be held at the World Championships in 2007.

12 INTERVIEW WITH LUKE WESTERLUND

Finally, Luke Westerlund, member of the American national Moguls team, reports on the developments in the sport and presents his view of things. He discusses the mutual influence of freeskiing and moguls and comes to the conclusion that no one sport is eclipsing the others, and they even strengthen and encourage each other.

In recent years, freeskiing has rocketed to the forefront of skiing popularity, taking the fortunes of many ex-mogul skiers along with it. The podiums of today's freeskiing competitions are populated almost entirely by ex-bumpers, guys like Tanner Hall, Candide Thovex, Mike Douglas, Pepe Fujus, Steele Spence, and Henrik Windstedt to name just a few.

It's no wonder that some mogul skiers have traded in anonymity and Olympic dreams for twintips and sponsor money. Freeskiing gives skiers a way to be part of the highly profitable and high profile action-sports movement. As freeskiing's popularity continues to grow, and freeskiing continues to be dominated by ex-mogul skiers, it stands to reason that mogul skiing must be losing its most talented athletes to freeskiing, right?

Skier: Luke Westerlund (USA). Photo: Gerhard Blöchl. Location: Inawashiro (JPN)

Wrong. The reality is that freeskiing and mogul skiing speak to different types of skiers, and both can continue to co-exist, even feed off each other.

First the hard facts: U.S. Ski and Snowboard Association Freestyle membership suffered a 4 % membership decline between 1999 and 2000. The decline might be attributed, in part, to the first burst of popularity when freeskiing hit the public's radar screen. But that theory doesn't necessarily hold water. Since 2000, as freeskiing has continued to grow, USSA freestyle membership has climbed at a steady 7.5 % year. Mogul skiing is alive and well in the United States, regardless of what New School skiing is doing.

I have been competing in moguls for 16 years and on the U.S. Ski Team for seven. For me, the decision to stay in moguls was a no-brainer. Mogul skiing is scored, and the judging is geared toward my strength – turns – while freeskiing is focused solely on air. Plus, in freeskiing, athletes' ability to market themselves appears to be as important as their skills, and that didn't interest me.

However, one of the guys I was coming up with had a different take on the situation. Evan Raps and I skied moguls together for about 10 years. Raps was always sick in the air. He spent his summers at the Lake Placid water ramps, developing his aerial skills. After one season on the U.S. Ski Team, Raps ditched his mogul skis to pursue a career in freeskiing.

"The number one factor in me quitting moguls was U.S. Ski Team politics," Raps says. "If I had been kept on the team, I probably would have kept skiing moguls." And like many ex-bumpers in freeskiing, Raps says he felt there was too little emphasis on having fun in mogul skiing. In freeskiing, Raps has gone on to claim a bronze medal at the 1999 Gravity Games and silver at the 2000 X-Games.

Gerhard Blöchl
Photo: Marco Hofstetter
Location: Golden Gym Maui (USA)

Raps' objections to moguls skiing – U.S. Ski Team politics and the seriousness of mogul training – are some of the most common reasons mogul skiers switch to freeskiing. Freeskiers session the parks with their buddies while mogul skiers train on a course with a coach watching. At the end of the day, freeskiers will likely be hanging out playing Playstation 2, while the mogul skiers are off to the gym.

The competitive atmosphere of mogul training fuels some skiers and the relaxed atmosphere of freeskiing fuels other skiers. Freeskiers also have a freedom to choose how and where they want to ski. They can compete, film, shoot for magazines or do demos. Mogul skiers' only opportunity for income or recognition is through competition. They must all go through their national ski federation in order to compete in World Cup events. For American skiers, this means abiding by the rules of the U.S. Team and the international organizations.

As skiing progresses, you'll see more kids doing both freeskiing and moguls. Most junior freestyle programs focus on both disciplines. Therefore, the talent pool isn't as specific to one discipline any more. This diversity is resulting in better, more versatile overall skiers. The formal training you get in moguls teaches you how to ski and compete. These basic skills have translated to successful careers of some of the world's best freeriders. As freeriding keeps pushing the level of skiing creativity, it's also fueling the different jumps that mogul skiers are throwing.

Currently, the diversity of freeskiing and mogul skiing is enlarging both talent pools and is ultimately increasing the level of both freeskiing and moguls.

APPENDIX

1   Links

Free Ski Magazines:
Freeskiing (USA)
Freeskier (USA)
Freeze (USA)
Powder (USA)
Poachers Freeski Magazine (GER)
Skiing – the next level (GER)
Bergstolz (GER)
X-Skier (GER)

Ski Magazines
Skiing (USA)
Ski (USA)
Mogul (JPN)
Planet Snow (GER)
DSV Aktiv (GER)
Ski Magazin (GER)

Events:

FIS Freestyle World Cups	www.fis-ski.com
Cham Jam	www.chamjam.com
Trifty Bump Bash	www.bumpbash.com
Ifsa X-Games	www.Ifsa.com
USSA Freestyle events	www.ussa.com
US Skiteam	www.usskiteam.com
German Freestyle Skiteam	www.freestyleteam.de
David Babic Web site (USA World Cup skier and author of this book)	www.davidbabic.com
Gerhard Blöchl Web site (German World Cup skier and author of this book)	www.bloechl.com

2 New School Dictionary

Air	Jump
Air Time	Flight phase
Alpine	Describes the ski disciplines of Slalom, Giant Slalom, Super-G and Downhill
Back country	Free terrain away from the marked slopes
Back flip	Backward somersault in the air (rotation around the latitudinal axis)
Bump	Mogul
Cliff Jump	Jump over a rock
Contest	Competition
Coping	The rim of the halfpipe
Drop in	Entering the halfpipe from the coping
Fakie	Moving backwards
Flat	The floor of the pipe
Flip	Forward, backward or sideways somersault in the air
Freeski	Skiing in free terrain, outside the marked slopes
Freestyle	The Olympic ski disciplines of moguls, aerials and the disciplines of skicross and ski halfpipe not yet included in the Olympics.
Gap Jump	Jump over road or wide ditch
Grab	Gripping the skis with a hand during a jump
Grinding	Sliding along a handrail or artificially prepared object

Halfpipe	Artificially prepared U-shaped pipe
Helicopter	360° turn around the body's longitudinal axis
Inverted	Describes overhead jumps
Kicker	Another term for a jump
Moguls	A slope with bumps
Off-Piste	Skiing outside of the ski area boundaries
Quarter Pipe	A halfpipe with only one wall
Spin	Turn around the body's longitudinal axis
Switch	Moving backwards
Table	Jump-off platform
Terrain park	Park artificially prepared with snow groomers with various jumps and rails for grinding.
Throw pad	A soft pad that can be tossed onto a trampoline to cushion an athlete's landing.
Tweak	Exhausting the anatomically possible movement radius in a grab.
Twintip	Special New School skis, which are shaped at both ends
Twister	Old freestyle jump in which the legs are extended at 90° to the side and then turned back to the starting position (usually done as a triple or quadruple twist)
Walls	Walls of a halfpipe

3   Photo Credits

Jacket design: Gerhard Blöchl
Cover photo: Patrick Reeves Photography
Back cover photo: Christoph Stark
Inside photos: see captions

4 Thanks

Our special thanks go to the Si-Q.de Team, especially to Claus Liebich, without whose support this book project would never have been published.

We would also like to thank the guest author Dr. Uwe Glatzmaier, Ruben Wellinger, Sven Küenle, Nathan Roberts and Luke Westerlund.

This book is also a visual work. So we would now like to thank the graphic designer Patrick Tschigg for putting together some of the photo sequences, as well as Tony Brey and Martin Trautmann for providing us with photographic material. In addition, we would like to especially thank the digital photography and graphic design work of Dan Starke and Patrick Reeves, both dear friends.

A big thanks also to Martina Ostermaier, who gave us valuable advice, encouragement, guidance and feedback during the preparation of the book. Our thanks also go to the Sports Scientist Doris Huber, who gave valuable support to our project.

A special thanks to my brother Kristopher Babic, for offering his editing advice, and providing us with a test subject for the jump progressions.

Last but not least, our thanks to the pupils of the Commercial High School Pasold Weisauer in Holzkirchen, who spent a day with us in the gym.

David, Armin and Gerhard

Ulli Heldt
Circuit Training – Tips for Success

Remember circuit training at school? Forget it! This book presents numerous possible variations of how to make a circuit be enjoyable, interesting and effective at the same time. The main emphasis here lies on strength, endurance, co-ordination and fun. *Tips for Success – Circuit Training* provides all sports teachers, trainers and instructors with several new ideas for lessons with different target groups.

168 pages, two-color print
6 photos, 75 figures
Paperback, 4 ^{1}/2" x 7"
ISBN 1-84126-028-2
£ 6.95 UK/$ 9.95 US
$ 12.95 CDN/€ 9.90

Alexander Jordan
Train your Back

This book will appeal to all those who want to take care of their backs – either at home, in a sports club, at school or in the gym. Sports leaders, teachers and coaches in particular will find new and varied teaching ideas. A focused pro-gramme offers varied and attractive exercises. The emphasis is placed on gentle strengthening gymnastics, supplemented by stretching and mobility programmes.

176 pages, two-color print
145 photos, 3 figures
Paperback, 5 ^{3}/4" x 8 ^{1}/4"
ISBN 1-84126-073-8
£ 12.95 UK/$ 17.95 US
$ 25.95 CDN/€ 16.90

MEYER & MEYER Sport | sales@m-m-sports.com | www.m-m-sports.com

Rieder/Fiala
Skiing Fitness
Conditioning Training for Ski Sports

104 pages, full-color print
65 photos and illustrations
Paperback, 5 ^{3}/4" x 8 ^{1}/4"
ISBN 1-84126-173-4
£ 9.95 UK/$ 14.95 US
$ 20.95 CDN/€ 14.95

The experienced skier does not take to the slopes without being fit. Fitness must be built up in preparation for the skiing season, and maintained during the winter so that particular goals may be achieved, and the risk of injury is reduced. Conditioning training should therefore be just as much a part of everyday training for off-piste skiers, freeriders and carvers as the honing of technical skills.

"Skiing Fitness"
- presents training programs for whole-body strengthening, mobility development, the reinforcement of the most used muscle groups and endurance training

- gives information on warming up and cooling down in training and on the slopes

- also gives recommendations for conditioning training on skis

- deals with the special characteristics of conditioning training for children and young people

MEYER & MEYER Sport | sales@m-m-sports.com | www.m-m-sports.com